KU-493-218

FOOD WORTH FIGHTING FOR

FROM FOOD RIOTS TO FOOD BANKS

Josh Sutton

PROSPECT BOOKS

2016

First published in 2016 in Great Britain and the United States
by Prospect Books, 26 Parke Road, London, SW13 9NG

© 2016 Josh Sutton

The author, Josh Sutton, asserts his right to be identified as author
of this work in accordance with the Copyright, Designs & Patents
Act 1988.

No part of this publication may be reproduced, stored in a retrieval
system, or transmitted in any form or by any means, electronic,
mechanical, photocopying, recording or otherwise, without the prior
permission of the copyright holder.

BRITISH LIBRARY CATALOGUING IN PUBLICATION DATA:
A catalogue entry of this book is available from the British Library.

Typeset and designed by Rebecca Gillieron and Catheryn Kilgarriff
in Adobe Garamond Pro

Cover design by Boff Whalley
All illustrations © 2016 Josh Sutton

ISBN 13 978-1-909248-48-9

Printed and bound by the Gutenberg Press, Malta.

CONTENTS

ACKNOWLEDGEMENTS

As well as drawing on the works of eminent historians such as E.P. Thompson, Hobsbawm, Rudé, Bohstedt, Sheldon and many others, I have used contemporary newspaper reports, local history groups and museums, together with folksong and ballad, to tell a tale of ordinary people doing extraordinary things. I clearly owe an enormous debt to those who have spent hours, days and years in meticulous research of their subjects. I've included a detailed bibliography, which may help readers with further research, and goes some way towards acknowledging the debt that I owe.

Thanks are due also to The Guild of Food Writers for support with travel costs during the research of this book.

In terms of personal thanks, and there are many who have gone out of their way to assist me, I would like to thank: My father Alan and my wife Anne-Marie for reading numerous revisions along the way. I would also like to thank the following who all took valuable time out of their schedules, often going to great lengths to reply to my somewhat rudimentary questions in person; Professor John Bohstedt of the University of Tennessee, Dr Naomi Hossain of the Institute of Development Studies, Professor Graham Riches of the University of British Columbia, Dr Carl Griffin of the University of Sussex, Dr Nick Mansfield of the University of Central Lancashire, Natalie Joelle, City University London. I am also indebted to Ben Haldene, Manager of Bradford Food Bank, who was more than generous in giving up his time and provided me with a valuable insight into the workings of his operation. Tristram Stuart was kind enough to share his opinion and thoughts on my comparison of food rioters past with the efforts of the Gleaning Network today. I am also grateful to Lydia of the Leeds branch of Foodcycle, for her time taken in answering my questions. Gill Watson and Adam Smith were kind in laughing off my description of them both as food rioters. Peter Higginbotham kindly granted permission to reproduce his 'Ballad of Captain Swing', and Grahame Moore and Alan Battersby were also kind enough to provide much useful information regarding food protest recorded in ballad and song. I would also like to thank David Matthews for a pleasant afternoon spent discussing the 'Newlyn Fish Riots' and the life of David's ancestor William Oats Stricke. Boff Whalley has to be thanked for his cover design, and I am also grateful to Casey Orr for the author photograph. Both Tom Jaine and Dr Bryce Evans kindly presented me with the opportunity to air chapters of this book on an unsuspecting public, and for that I am most grateful. Finally, I am also hugely indebted to Geoff Tansey, both for his time spent one sunny morning discussing my project, but also for his work on the open resource 'Food Systems Academy' (www.foodsystemsacademy. org.uk), a highly valuable resource for those interested in furthering their understanding of the nature of our food system.

It ought to go without saying, that while all of those above have helped me in my research, the views presented in this book are mine alone and do not necessarily reflect the opinions of those listed.

PREFACE

Some years ago, I worked as a labourer in deepest rural Wiltshire. My wages at the time were one hundred and seventy five pounds, and two rabbits per week. The rabbits weren't written into my contract, I didn't even have a contract, but my boss insisted that I should benefit from his sideline of nocturnal pest control for the local farmers. Though the freezer at home was fast filling with rabbits (two rabbits per week is a lot for a young single fellow to get through), on the weeks that they weren't available, I found I would miss them. It felt as though I had been short-changed; it was akin to having my wages docked. Compensation came, from time to time, with 'a nice bit of wild venison', which my boss had accidentally managed to shoot while out hunting rabbits, so things probably balanced out in the end. However, as well as teaching me the finer points of skinning, butchering and cooking Leporidae, this direct relationship with food left me with a lasting appreciation of the importance of its availability. Perhaps more importantly, it gave me an insight into the effect that a lack of available food can have on the morale of the village labourer.

It is through the plight of the village labourer, the fisherman, the artisan and other working class men and women, that the story of *Food Worth Fighting For* unfolds. It's a story about hunger, poverty, camaraderie, woe and joy. Above all it is about communities, and in the case of chapter six, a whole country working together to feed themselves and each other. It's about a demand for change to a food system, which came about largely as a result of the Industrial Revolution, and one which even today fails the most vulnerable in our society. *Food Worth Fighting For* is a story about food riots and the struggle to put food on the table at home. It looks at food poverty in Britain today and makes the bold suggestion that the ethos of the food riot is still very much alive. Though many of the riots, disturbances and struggles discussed in the following pages were born of poverty, it is by no means the case that all were. This is not a book about poverty per se, rather it is an attempt to illustrate what I see as a continuum of struggle, one which has endured for over two centuries. The forms of that struggle have altered over the years, and although the levels of violence may have abated, I believe that the food riot is still with us today, however it is just that it has taken on a different guise. In many cases, I believe that the food charity workers of today are symbolic of the food rioters of the past. Today's struggle is more of a fight than a riot. In modern parlance, the word 'riot' conjures images of individuals rampaging through burning streets, their identities obscured by hoodies and makeshift masks. Poor quality CCTV images often portray scenes of looting amid an avaricious scramble for consumer goods, one in the eye for law and order. I believe that today's images of rioters are a far cry from those that might have been available in previous centuries. A riot in days gone by had a broader meaning. To a certain extent, its definition has been hijacked by modernity. Think of a riot of colour, a riot of emotion, or to borrow a line from one of my favourite songwriters, 'cudgelling the air with a riot of a sound'.[1] The connotations of rioting went far beyond mere lawbreaking and opened up possibilities for celebration and revelry.

With over a million people dependent on food banks, and an all party parliamentary group (APPG) set up to examine food poverty and hunger in Britain in 2014, it struck me that today's food system is still failing a huge swathe of British society. How is it that school teachers in modern Britain can raise concerns about their pupils' capacity to learn, because children are going to school hungry in the morning? How do we explain the explosion in the numbers of local and national charities, as well as individuals, offering food aid to the less well off in this country? Some of those concerns were reflected by the Bishop of Truro, Tim Thornton in the introduction to the report 'Feeding Britain', published by the APPG in December of 2014:

> The issues people face relating to hunger and food poverty are exacerbated and highlighted because there are hardly any of the ways and means that once did exist for people to support each other. We believe that the rise in the use of food banks is a sign of the breakdown of this core value in our society.[2]

And the Archbishop of Canterbury, Justin Welby, said in the *Guardian* in December 2015 that it was '"a tragedy" that hunger still existed in the UK in the 21st century' and he 'praised the work of charity food banks which he said were "striving to make life bearable for people who are going hungry"'.

The leader of the church of England placed some of the blame for hunger on the government, singling out 'unnecessary problems' caused by bureaucratic delays in welfare benefit payments and sanctions – financial penalties imposed by job centres – which left vulnerable claimants without money for food for weeks on end.

In an age where the vast majority of us carry out the weekly shop under one roof, we seem to have lost faith in the market place. Skips full of surplus food deliberately spoiled to prevent 'scavengers', the horsemeat scandal of 2013, and more recently the examples of creative accountancy at supermarket chain, Tesco, have shaken public confidence in our supermarkets. Yet rather than take to the streets to demand change, the majority of us continue to queue at the express checkout counter, tempted, and bought off with two-for-one offers and a price guarantee. Consumers and food producers alike, have become unsuspecting collateral damage in a never-ending supermarket price war as our food system has developed and grown, driven largely by commercial avarice. We have become casualties of a capitalist culture that undermines our right to food, a right which arguably dates back to the signing of the Magna Carta, and was more recently set out in the Universal Declaration of Human Rights in 1948. Our food system today has given rise to the paradox of soaring obesity rates, while others go hungry. Food poverty has hit the headlines. How can it be that a pint of milk can cost as little as 58p, yet families the length and breadth of Britain are referred to food banks on an almost daily basis?

Food Worth Fighting For is an attempt to portray the struggle for food in this country as a continuum, emanating from a rich tradition of food riots, many of which appear to have been forgotten somewhat, or at very least conveniently overlooked. The poor in Britain have been engaged in a fight for food for hundreds of years, in times of dearth, individuals and communities have rallied in an attempt to ensure that people do not go hungry. In modern austerity Britain, this practise continues through the growing 'industry' of food charity. A key difference today, however, appears to be that rather than hungry people themselves organizing such relief, it appears to be others organizing on their behalf.

'We'd rather be hanged, than starve to death' was a popular refrain 200 years ago. It was a motif which I encountered time and time again during my research, which took me back to the late eighteenth century and beyond. This was a period in which we had a very different relationship with food and those who produced it, by comparison to today. I found a story, which I believe is as relevant in the twenty-first century, as it was hundreds of years ago, if not more so. I found circumstances affecting the poor of the eighteenth and nineteenth centuries which might well be recognized today, amid the present government's cutbacks on the welfare state and it's current onslaught against the poor. What follows is the story of the food riot in Britain, and how those riots have evolved in response to tackling hunger over the past two centuries.

The importance and availability of food in our daily lives has shifted, ebbed and flowed, over the years. Busy modern lives, with work, school and other commitments have lead to the apparent demise of the regular family meal. Our eating habits have changed. Where food once formed a key foundation of the economy, and was even used in some cases (including my own) as currency or wages, food today has become a mere commodity, one among many being traded along with gold, copper and oil. Food price inflation in the UK has been running higher than the general inflation rate since 2007, driven chiefly by global commodity prices, exchange rates and oil prices.

The cultural significance of food in Britain has arguably been on the wain over the years, health and safety concerns for the Cheese Rollers of Coopers Hill in Gloucestershire, for example, have recently put paid to an age old tradition, one which celebrated the lengths to which we might go to get hold of this much-loved foodstuff. In a number of European countries however, the link between food and cultural tradition has been maintained. In some cases, the notion of a food fight has been preserved, entered the public realm and become established as a cultural pastime, ritualistic in its recurrence and attracting large numbers of participants often from abroad. La Tomatina, a festival held annually in the Spanish city of Buñol, appears to have its roots set in rebellion, as youngsters allegedly excluded from participating in an annual parade through the city, sought to join the festivities many years ago. A town of 9,000 inhabitants is besieged by up to 30,000 visitors at the end of August each year. The festival has become so popular that city authorities now limit numbers and revellers must pay to throw tomatoes at each other in the street.

A similar event takes place in the Italian city of Ivrea. As with La Tomatina in Spain, the detailed origins of the ritual are unclear but appear born of a defiance of authority. Oranges are thrown by participants, in celebration of the besting of a local tyrant. Again, the event attracts a crowd of participants from beyond the city limits, though one would imagine that the queue to be pelted with tomatoes would be considerably longer than those waiting in line to be bombarded with whole oranges.

One of the appealing draws of a food fight is that they appear to cock a snook at authority. Whether it's a sustained campaign to persuade governments to alter their fishing practises, or the symbolic preservation of a custom, a food fight entices others to join in, to revel in disdain. The riots and food fights described in the following pages, however, were born of more pressing circumstances.

As the importance of food has shifted from the centre to the periphery of our economy, and into the realms of investment bankers where it now balances portfolios as well as diets, so too it appears, has the degree to which we will fight for our food in Britain. Consumers are in danger of becoming ever more distant and removed from the source of food. It is of little surprise, as boneless, skinless, cellophane wrapped parcels of meat on the supermarket shelves leave little clue as to the origins, let alone the species of animal inside. The colour coded packaging, green for lamb, blue for pork and red for beef, is often the only distinction and means of us knowing whether our evening meal once sported horns or a curly tail. To me there is a danger, that as we become less concerned for the provenance and more so with the price of our food; our stomach for a fight disappears. Bloated with injected additives, anaesthetised by agronomics, it seems more difficult than ever to take up the struggle, but perhaps I am wrong.

The advent of social media has greatly increased our capacity to participate in a food fight these days. In the UK, over 31.5 million people have a Facebook account, and some 15 million people have a Twitter account. It is now easier than ever to join in with a food fight, and both Twitter and Facebook serve as open recruiting grounds for participants. Relieved of the inconvenience of having to take to the street, for many of us the desire for justice and fair play can be sated with the simple click of a mouse. The term 'food fight' itself appears to be back in vogue. Popular televised campaigns by celebrity chefs and food writers have recently attracted tens of thousands of viewers and drawn new recruits to the ranks of Britain's food protestors. They've even helped change the law in some cases. Jamie Oliver's 'School Dinners', and 'Food Revolution' campaigns, Hugh Fearnley-Whittingstall's 'Fish Fight' took up the cause for a sensible approach to how we procure and prepare our food in the twenty-first century.

The age of petition is with us. For those in centuries past, the struggle was very much a physical one and it is largely thanks to their efforts that the majority of Britons, until recently at least, were able to sit down to a full plate at meal times.

Food riots were common across England in the eighteenth and nineteenth centuries, and were born of necessity and hunger, rather than mere antagonism. Some historians hold that serious rioting was the means whereby English society sought to achieve radical change as it moved towards a new equilibrium.[2] The late eighteenth, and nineteenth centuries saw sweeping change across Britain. The changes were to have a dynamic impact on our relationship with food and our means of obtaining it. The changes, which came with industrialization, with war and with competing economic theories, saw men women and children take to the streets of our towns and villages.

> COME, neighbours, no longer be patient and quiet
> Come let us go kick up a bit of a riot;
> I am hungry, my lads, but I've little to eat,
> So we'll pull down the mills, and seize all the meat:
> I'll give you good sport, boys, as ever you saw,
> So a fig for the Justice, a fig for the law.

So goes the opening verse of a popular, controversial ballad, titled 'The Riot', which dates from the early part of the nineteenth century. The controversy appears in the form of a dialogue between two fellows, as 'Jack Anvil' warns 'Tom Hod' of the dangers and consequences of rioting. The final verse is clearly a win for the authorities of law and order:

> Then before I'm induced to take part in a Riot,
> I'll ask this short question - What shall I get by it?
> So I'll e'en wait a little till cheaper the bread,
> For a mittimus hangs o'er each Rioter's head:
> And when of two evils I'm ask'd which is best,
> I'd rather be hungry than be hang'd, I protest.

Ballads such as this, published by Morrison of Perth as a 'broadside' pamphlet, reflect a call for calm as its subtitle claims, 'Half a loaf is better than no bread'. Its very existence indicates that rioting was commonplace, and that steps to dissuade the public from doing so were necessary. The thirteen verses are peppered with jibes, and ridicule for 'those blockheads who rush into riot' and urge would-be lawbreakers to make do and be grateful for what they have. The Ballad runs counter to the sentiment of that popular refrain, 'we'd rather be hanged than starve to death'. The notion that food rioters had nothing to loose, and that direct action was their only recourse is one that features heavily in these pages.

Food riots in England were not uncommon as far back as the sixteenth century. In his *Atlas of Rural Protest*, Andrew Charlesworth documents episodes of food associated social unrest from 1548, right up until 1900. I have chosen to focus on food fights and protests, which date from the late eighteenth century, as this is arguably a period in which began a series of sweeping changes and developments which went on to shape modern society as we know it. These developments include the expansion of the Enclosure Movements, the Corn Laws, the onset of the Industrial Revolution, the Poor Law reforms, the development of the workhouse system, and the development and improvement of transport and communication links throughout the country. It was a time of flux, as populations moved from the country to the cities, beginning the process of urbanization and arguably changing the geography of this country forever.

What is perhaps most remarkable about the food riots of the eighteenth and nineteenth centuries is the manner in which they were carried out. Though without doubt prompted through fear of starvation as well as a disdain for the authorities at the time, plunder was uncommon. In many cases, rioters didn't steal food, they sought to fix a fair price and proceeds were more often than not returned to owners. Rioters were battling for what they perceived as their 'rights'. In many cases they enjoyed the support, respect and encouragement from a broader public, which sometimes included the local magistrate and other figures of authority. Concessions were gained and made, in market places and guildhalls up and down the country, which often lent an air of legitimacy to the protest. In what he describes as the 'moral economy' of the crowd, the historian E.P. Thompson has observed that men and women gathered in crowds were often informed by the belief that they were defending traditional rights or customs.[3] This sense of righteousness must have spurred them on, as in a period of 270 years up until 1820 there were more than 700 food riots in England.[4]

The fact that riots and disturbances were often quick to spread across counties to neighbouring towns and villages also appears to lend weight to a perceived legitimacy among the participants. To a degree it also reflects the nature and structure of society at the time. Communication among the would-be rioters was greatly aided by the fact that farm labour, for example, was often drawn from a pool of workers which spread over numerous towns and villages. Handbills and posters informing of intentions of action, and offering warnings to corrupt tradesmen and merchants, were often nailed to church doors and displayed in market places. As rational responses to real grievances, rather than mere outbreaks of hooliganism, riots were often seen by the authorities as an unavoidable symptom of the distribution of wealth. In many ways, they were seen therefore as par for the course. This clearly presented a number of problems for the authorities, usually local magistrates, engaged in trying to quell the riots. Over the years, we see striking differences in the degree of severity with which punishments are metered out to convicted prisoners. In some cases, I believe that this has to do with an innate sympathy, among some of the harbingers of justice, as they were all too aware of the often appalling conditions, under which many of those convicted were living. In other cases, leniency appears to have been granted, where concerns for the social repercussions of sentencing have been expressed.

On occasions when troops were called, it would often take a number of days for them to get to the scene. Even on arrival, their action could be ineffectual, particularly among volunteer soldiers, as they themselves often lived under conditions similar to those they were supposed to suppress. Some soldiers were less than enthusiastic in going about their duties. Efforts to arrest rioters could also be hampered by further protest and a widespread reluctance, among the populace, to 'turn in' any fugitives. Even after sentence had been passed, supportive communities were known to hinder the progress of justice, in the town of Ely in 1816, for example, the authorities were forced to send out of town for a cart to bear condemned food rioters to the gallows, as none from the town would lend theirs.[5]

That people were prepared to work together, in a collective approach, as they took to the streets in protest also strengthens the argument for commonality among the crowd. This commonality forms a key part of what historian E.P. Thompson described as 'the moral economy of the crowd', an economy based around a perceived set of 'historical rights' derived through common values and norms. At times, as those values and norms were challenged by rapidly changing circumstances, communities reacted. Whilst the argument that, 'that's how we do things round here' might lack discursive prowess in a debate, it none the less remains as a given within any community, and might be used by that community as a means of resisting change.

As the social, political and agricultural geography of the country began to develop over years, so too did the demands and aspirations of food rioters. In particular, the shift in Britain from a largely agrarian society towards one of an industrial, wage-based, society brought with it new demands from rioters which, in addition to those for bread and fair prices, posed a greater threat to governments at the time. New demands for better wages and working conditions alongside affordable food were now being made in an increasingly industrialized and mechanized society. Protests took on a more violent air as other movements such as the Luddites and the Swing rioters directed their anger at newfangled machinery and property, rather than just people. Ten years of revolution in France at the end of the eighteenth century brought worry and concerns to the establishment in Britain. By the mid nineteenth century, those fears were once again unleashed as a series of uprisings swept across much of Europe in 1848. There was genuine concern in parliament that the country would succumb to revolution.

In recounting these episodes in our history, it is practically impossible to see food fights as anything other then a straight battle between those who 'have', and those who 'have not'. To put it another way, food riots and protest emerged as the result of a class war between rich and poor, and this is a war which continues today. To dismiss the actions of rioters merely as those of violent criminals would be to mask the achievements of those involved. Even as recently as 2007 – 2012, as the Manor House allotment holders of East London (and I would argue that those involved were 'food rioters of the modern age') struggled to hold on to their vegetable patches in the face of the onslaught of the mighty Olympic Park Machine, food fighters were seen by some as a disruptive rabble bent on wreaking havoc in the path of progress, spoiling it for the others. Through exploring these, and other chapters in history, I hope that I might build a picture of a long forgotten tradition, of a right to expect and demand, and fight for affordable food.

For me, this examination of food riots and food poverty serves a purpose, highlighting similar struggles, which continue in the twenty-first century. In choosing to recount these tales in sequence I'm attempting to put seemingly isolated events such as the 'Gloucester Bread Riots' of 1766, into perspective. The perspective reflects an overlooked continuum of struggle dating back hundreds of years. In an era of restricted suffrage, and in the absence of the modern democracy, which helps define today's political arena, rioting in the eighteenth and nineteenth centuries, in particular, was a means of engaging the state in a political dialogue. In many cases it brought results, price setting being a good example. E.P. Thompson maintained that the word 'riot' was not big enough to encompass the complexity of the food fights, which I describe in the following pages. Given the diversity of factors that drove people to riot in the first place, I'm inclined to agree. Clearly as the political arena has opened up, the nature of the food fight has changed over the years, as has the arena in which they are fought. From the market squares and Butter crosses of English cities, towns and villages, to the byte size jaws of the world wide web, the tradition of the food riot is still alive and kicking, it's just that from time to time we fail to see it for what it really is. People are still struggling to put food on the table at home, while others actively campaign in an effort to make sure that the poor in Britain don't go hungry.

In telling this story, I have attempted to use the popular social media of the time. Folksong, ballads and poetry help tell the tale, often describing the conditions under which people toiled. Where possible, I've named individuals and described events recorded in newspapers and county records. I wanted to make it personal, in a bid to reintroduce a popular history to a broader audience. It is a history which has been lost, but one which is beginning to re-emerge, and will hopefully encourage people to re-examine the trust we place in the market driven food system we have today.

END NOTES

1. From 'The field of the cloth of gold' by Nick Harper (2007).
2. Shelton, *English hunger and industrial disorders*, p.3.
3. Thompson, E.P. *The Moral Economy of the English Crowd*.
4. Bohstedt, J. *The Politics of Provisions* p.2.
5. Johnson, C. *An Account of the Ely and Littleport Riots*.

INTRODUCTION

A Changing Landscape

Our Sovereign Lord the King chargeth and commandeth all persons, being assembled, immediately to disperse themselves, and peaceably to depart to their habitations, or to their lawful business, upon the pains contained in the act made in the first year of King George, for preventing tumults and riotous assemblies. God Save the King!

So states the proclamation that would have been familiar to almost everyone who took part in many of the riots and disturbances described in the following pages. Having heard these words, often read by a local magistrate or other representative of the authorities, those gathered were given just one hour in which to disperse. Failure to do so was considered a felony and accordingly carried the death penalty, though clearly prison sentences and transportation were used as a deterrent and punishment too. The proclamation forms a key part of the Riot Act of 1715, and for those engaged in tumult and riotous assembly, it would have marked the end of the fun and games, or at least signified that the end was indeed nigh. The Riot Act gave a clear indication of the state's attitude towards law and order. It redefined an act of 'riot' as assembly, rather than merely causing damage to persons or property. Its deliberate heightening of the element of force signified a determination to deal decisively with popular disorder.[1] By 'upgrading' the gathering in unlawful assembly to an act of felony, as opposed to one of misdemeanour, it marked a significant change in the way that riots were dealt with in law.

Social unrest has a long history in Britain; from the signing of the Magna Carta through the civil war right up to the actions of Emmeline Pankhurst and the Suffragette Movement, you could argue that modern Britain was built and shaped by its people kicking up a bit of a fuss. In many of the uprisings and disturbances over the years, food has been central in protesters' concerns. The majority of these outbreaks and disturbances occurred with regular frequency during the whole of the eighteenth century, with individual periods of unrest often lasting more than a year at a time. The frequency of food riots in Britain, however, declined in the early part of the nineteenth century, so that by the middle of that century, as the Industrial Revolution reshaped the majority of trades and industry in this country, widespread popular protest was more often seen as a labour dispute as opposed to a fight to put food on the table at home.

The circumstances under which men and women would take part in food riots in Britain were, and are to this day, both diverse and dynamic. Whilst individual participants might have their own reasons for joining in, a food riot by its very nature presents a collective response to a situation, and more often than not, carries with it a clear set of objectives. Those objectives, for example, could relate to supply and distribution of food, as well as the price of such. Many of the 'grain riots', those, which took place in the county of Gloucestershire and much of the west of England in 1766, were in particular concerned with farmers' practices of withholding grain in the hope of commanding a higher price at market. At times, removal of food supplies to other parts of the county, or even outside of the county, would cause concern among the local inhabitants who may have seen vital supplies slipping beyond their grasp. The price of food fluctuated greatly at the overlap of the eighteenth and nineteenth centuries. Crop failures, inclement weather and the wars with France, and a corresponding need to victual whole armies, all had a detrimental effect on the affordability of food at home. The Corn Laws, brought in at this time to protect the price of grain were something of a double-edged sword. By upholding the prices of domestic supplies, and insisting upon the domestic supply being exhausted before imported corn was permitted to be sold at market, the authorities at the time of course enjoyed the support of farmers and corn merchants, but were the subject of the wrath of those who found the price of a loaf beyond their means. Affordability, of course, is a factor, which can affect the whole gamut of society, though it is fair to assume a higher impact would be felt by the poor and those on lower incomes. Whilst those at the very margins of society, the homeless and destitute, may have participated in food riots, it is of interest that prosecuting authorities went to great lengths to demonstrate that many of the rioters were far from destitute and displayed among them a diverse range of skills and occupations. It is as if attempts were made by the authorities at the time to dismiss the notion that food riots were an act of desperation, and that by taking into account the rioters' professions, their acts might be seen as being driven by avarice rather than hunger. The fact that times were so hard that even skilled artisans as well as common labourers felt the need to riot appears to have been overlooked. Records from the special Assizes held to try those arrested often detailed occupation and income of those in the dock. Historian John Archer, writing as recently as 2000, has observed that protesters were typically respectable members of the community, and reports of outsiders causing mayhem were rare. He also observes the occasional complicity of militias and those called in to deal with a disturbance, citing an example in the county of Devon, where local militia refused to act against rioters during the 1790s.[2] The militiamen were either sympathetic with the rioters, or perhaps fearful of any later repercussions of intervention. Militia were, after all, drawn from local communities, and hence recruits would more than likely have an in depth understanding of the conditions under which common people lived.

That food riots were more frequent in the past, than in recent years, appears to stem from a number of significant factors, namely a number of sweeping changes which altered forever both the physical and political geography of Britain. These changes provide an important context within which the food riots described here took place. Legislation such as the Enclosure Acts (dating from the fifteenth century), the Game Laws (emerging from the 'forest laws' following the Norman invasion), the Corn Laws (1815), the Poor Laws (dating from the sixteenth century and with significant legislation in 1815 and 1834), have all played their part in widening the gap between rich and poor, and engineering riot. Social custom and religious belief as well as world wars and competing economic theories have also been implicated in contributing to food riots. It is clear that no one thing could be singled out as a catalyst for a food fight, but a brief examination of some of the key factors will help to demonstrate that while food riots may often appear spontaneous, each was born of a genuine concern.

The Enclosure Movements have had the most far-reaching effect on food production in Britain. Over a period of several centuries, beginning in the fifteenth century, once common land was parcelled up and annexed by rich land owners in a quasi-legitimate process, which bore all the legal prowess of a dog marking its territory with the cock of a hind leg. 'Commoners' farming narrow strips of land, and those with traditional grazing rights on the common were deprived of their means of growing and rearing their own food. In some cases, it is possible to see the expansion of enclosures occurring in tandem with the advance of technology and it is often argued that enclosure was a necessary phenomenon in order to facilitate the development of modern farming methods. The enclosure of common land is arguably the most significant factor contributing to the proliferation of food riots in the following centuries.

Enclosure has been around for a very long time, and it is reasonably safe to say that it has had its fair share of critics since its inception.

In 1516, Sir Thomas More, Lord Chancellor to Henry VIII, brought his concerns over the impact of enclosure upon the English peasant, to the attention of the authorities. More had observed how some noblemen, gentlemen and unscrupulous abbots had a tendency to demolish homes which fell within their new enclosures, and would evict the occupants without so much as a by your leave. A year later, a commission was established in an effort to protect the interests of the peasant. Whilst recognizing some of the concerns aired by More, the commission was limited in its powers to deal with the manor in which enclosures came about.³ This may of course be testament to More's influence over the King, or perhaps lack of it, as he was to lose his head shortly afterwards for refusing to recognize the King's position as head of the church.

In replacing the old medieval system of semi-communal open field farming and affecting the very way in which farmers and land owners interact with the earth, enclosure has done much to inform the structure of society over the years. It led to depopulation in many rural areas and has shaped the very towns, cities and villages we live in today. The enclosure of common land had a lasting and detrimental effect on those who once made use of it, not merely for grazing livestock, or gathering and cutting fuel for cooking and heating, but in some cases for building homes on it.

A significant and rapid expansion of enclosure took place in the latter part of the eighteenth and early nineteenth centuries. Historian W.E. Tate, writing in 1967, describes an almost amusing and condescending rhetoric, which was used at the time in espousing its merits. To me it sheds light on the imperious nature of enclosure, and reiterates the guile and determination needed for those who would resist their progress. Enclosure was clearly presented as bringing moral as well as economic benefits.

The undeserving poor, especially the insubordinate squatters, living in riotous squalor in their tumbledown hovels on the common, would prosper morally and economically if they were compelled to do regular work for an employer. Everyone in the parish would gain by the increase of employment in hedging, ditching, fencing, draining and by the fall in rates which was confidently expected as soon as the common land had ceased to form a constant attraction to all the beggars, wastrels and drunkards in the district.[4]

The derogatory and pejorative language used in this passage serves to reinforce some sort of perceived 'given' that the poor ought be driven towards labour. If this was the ethos at the time, as indeed it was, it is easy to see the direction in which any Poor Law reform might take in later years. The nature in which enclosures were made, and legitimized, changed with time. During the medieval period, enclosure was granted by Court Baron, one of the lowest law courts in England, which dealt with matters under the jurisdiction of the Lord of the Manor. Land grabs by lords of the manor, and other major landowners, were effectively sanctioned by the very act of enclosure itself. The lack of formal ritual or legitimate procedure at this time clearly caused some concern among those evicted from common land. In 1549, a Norfolk-based tenant farmer named Robert Kett sided with protesting commoners and led a rebellion of some considerable size, one which was eventually put down by the army under the Earl of Warwick. By the seventeenth century, enclosure was carried out by Chancery, or Exchequer Decree. It was still very much a local affair and bore all the hallmarks of the 'done deal' of previous years. By the latter half of the eighteenth century, enclosure was brought about by private act of parliament. The 'legality' of enclosure was being enhanced in an age where the power of the legislature was rapidly overshadowing that of the monarch and that of the judicature, so it made clear sense from a legal point of view.[5]

As the rate of enclosure grew under its new parliamentary legitimacy, so too did the level of protest from those opposing the acts. Serious uprisings against enclosure were commonplace down the centuries. During the English Revolution, the Diggers, lead by Gerrard Winstanley, began cultivating land on St George's Hill in Surrey, where they proclaimed a free Commonwealth with a manifesto that held that:

> England is not a Free people, till the Poor that have no Land, have a free allowance to dig and labour the Commons, and so live as Comfortably as the Landlords that live in their Inclosures.[6]

Despite encroaching legislation over the following years, defiance remained as commoners continued to work, hunt and gather fuel on once common land. The Black Act of 1723 was a response by Prime Minister Walpole, to what was now seen as brazen acts of poaching on privately owned and crown owned woodlands. The act brought with it draconian penalties for those caught poaching and served to further resentment and opposition among the commoners. Historian Simon Fairlie describes a bold, to say the least, act of defiance in the actions of the leader of a masked gang who killed seven deer out of the Bishop's Park at Farnham, and then rode in triumph, parading them through Farnham market the following morning.[7] Opponents to enclosures also included some farmers and landowners as well as the landless poor. In 1826, the journalist and political reformist William Cobbett described his dismay over the proposed enclosure of Waltham Chase in rural Hampshire:

> one of the finest pieces of timberland in the whole kingdom, going to be cut up into miserable clay fields, for no earthly purpose but that of gratifying the stupid greediness of those who think that they must gain, if they add to the breadth of their private fields.[8]

To say that enclosure fuelled a resentment towards the authorities that carried them out would be an understatement. The animosity towards enclosures is clear in a popular verse from around 1821:

> The fault is great in man or woman
> Who steals a goose from off a common,
> But what can plead that man's excuse,
> Who steals a common from a goose.[9]

By the nineteenth century, enclosure had shifted from a private to a general act of parliament, in part as a response to a series of bad harvests as well as the enhanced nutritional needs of the nation's army and navy, brought about by the Napoleonic Wars. In a series of moves, which were echoed later by the War Agricultural Executive Committees formed during the First and Second World Wars, enclosure was promoted by the government as a 'necessity' in the effort to produce more food for the nation, and in particular, food for the forces engaged in fighting for the country.

The enclosures left in their wake a residual charge throughout the British countryside, a slow burning disdain, which from time to time would resurface and serve to add more than just a drop of fuel to the flames of a nascent food fight. The 'privatization' of once public amenities is a practise which has continued well into the modern day, and is one which has clearly affected the public's ability to make use of those amenities, particularly in regard to the price of fuel needed for heating and cooking in the modern home. The similarities between 'privatization' and the enclosure movements, to me at least, appear too striking to not warrant a mention and the threat of the new enclosures, generated around the intellectual property rights associated with the shift towards use of genetic modification in the food system, opens up a whole new arena for a food fight, but more of that later.

The expansion of enclosure acts between 1760 and 1820, of course runs in tandem with the Industrial Revolution in England. The appropriation of common land was often seen, or described at least, as necessary to facilitate the onset of modernity. To put it another way, the needs aroused by the Industrial Revolution in urban areas demanded a corresponding agrarian revolution in the countryside.[10] Clearly the Industrial Revolution had its detractors, and in turn prompted protest within the urban industrial arena. The shift from a largely rural agrarian society to an increasingly urban wage-based market economy, in which the poor had naught but their labour to offer as a means of survival, became even more difficult as technological advancements began to abrogate the need for human labour. It would be difficult to talk about food riots without a mention of the

Industrial Revolution and the role it played in exacerbating poverty and contributing to what Hobsbawm called 'a high wind of social discontent,' which spread across much of the country at the time. Collective anger against mill owners in the textile trades came about as new labour saving inventions were introduced into the workplace. The Luddites are perhaps the most famous group of protesters during this period. Protests and destruction of machinery broke out in the growing industrial cities of the Midlands and spread to the mills of Lancashire and Yorkshire between 1811 and 1817. The movement was named after a mythical character, Ned Ludd, and the intentions and aims of the Luddites are well documented by historians.

In the countryside just a few years later, agricultural workers turned their attention, and displayed a similar animosity towards threshing machines, which too were seen as putting people out of work. The 'Swing Riots' of 1830 sit well within this compendium of 'food fights' as the machines which were destroyed, and the people who went about their destruction were directly involved in the manufacture of food. It is interesting to note that, similarly to the Luddite movement, the 'Swing Riots' were 'led' by a mythical character, 'Captain Swing'. That each movement, as well as others throughout history, should choose to appoint a mythical, almost infallible leader, and one which takes on a number of benevolent characteristics (a 'Robin Hood' like championing of the poor for example) serves to suggest, if not demonstrate a perceived common set of ideals and norms among the protesters.

Another well established collective response to those who might challenge common norms and ideals, took the form of 'Rough Music'. Seated deep within British folklore, rather than solely a manifestation in reaction to the 'high wind of social discontent', 'Rough Music' was often given as a collective punishment for a member of the community that had in some way erred or broken 'the rules'. Similar rituals are described throughout Europe, the French '*charivari*', or '*scampamente*' in Italian, '*katzenmuzik*' in Germany.[11] A crowd would gather outside the home of a wrongdoer and proceed to deliver a cacophony played upon old pots and pans, hunting horns and other discordant instruments of various descriptions. The offender would be publicly shamed in front of the whole community. Variations of this practice were to be found throughout England during the eighteenth and nineteenth centuries, and might go by differing names, such as a 'Skimmington ride', or a 'ran tan'. The ritual of 'rough music' has been represented in art and literature over the years. Thomas Hardy wrote of an early nineteenth-century Skimmington in *The Mayor of Casterbridge* (1886). Hogarth's 1726 engraving 'Hudibras encounters the Skimmington' depicts a crowd in full swing chastizing a husband and wife amid accusations of adultery. It takes no stretch of the imagination to consider some of the rituals, practices and ethos of 'rough music' being applied during some of the food fights and riots described in these pages. That there was an established practise and custom of a crowd gathering to vent disapproval in a collective manner must surely have relevance in the case of the food riot. Indeed actions of a similar nature are described in accounts of the 'Bread and Beer Riots' of East Anglia in 1816, where rioters would gather outside the homes of local dignitaries blamed for the austere conditions in which unhappy rioters often found themselves.[12]

If food riots are to be seen, in part, as a response to poverty and deprivation, then it is clear that successive governments declined to adopt effective prophylactic measures. It is as if food riots were an accepted symptom of a political system in flux, a tolerated hazard of a developing market economy. As far as the poor were concerned, expropriation through legislation was a given. From the 'forest law' introduced by William the Conqueror to the 'Black Act' of 1723, the taking of animals from the wild was largely forbidden and carried severe penalties which meant that those caught might face imprisonment, execution or transportation. Enclosure (as well as the Industrial Revolution itself) had done much to 'corral' the poor into larger towns and cities in search of food, shelter and employment. For those that remained in the countryside, it not only took away their right to graze what animals they may have had upon the common, but removed the right to gather wood for heating and cooking fuel. 'Fuel poverty' is clearly not a new concept, it plays a significant role in today's food fight and is a point we shall return to a little later in this book.

The capacity for the poor to feed themselves was further eroded with what became known as 'the great gleaning case of 1788'. Until this date, the tradition of gleaning was taken as a customary right by the poor. In a practice which arguably dates back to biblical times, villagers enjoyed the right to 'glean' the fields after harvest, gathering crops left over. It was a process carried out with ritual and tradition and formed what would have been seen as an important feature in the agricultural calendar, and one which made a significant contribution to the larders of the poor. Some communities would elect a 'Gleaning Queen' whose job was to oversee the proceedings and ensure that all got an equal share of the pickings. Following the harvest, farmers would carry out a final gathering of their crop as they sought to maximize the yield from the fields. Once the farmers, or landowners, were satisfied that their returns were secured, they would throw open the fields to the village gleaners, more often than not the womenfolk and children of the community. This was a practise governed with strict code, to the extent that the signal for gleaning to commence was governed by the presence of the 'guard sheaf'. In a fascinating account of the ancient practise of gleaning in the county of Essex, and using W.E. Bates' 1938 tale *The Gleaner*, as well as interviews with locals with living memory of having practised gleaning themselves, Stephen Hussey details the experience of gleaners and gives an account of the practise continuing right up until the 1950s.[13] The 'guard sheaf' was a single sheaf of corn left standing by the farmer to indicate that he had yet to finish gathering his own crop. Once the guard sheaf was removed, then gleaning could commence. As well as the guard sheaf, the ringing of the parish church bell, the gleaning bell, was another signal that the fields were open for gleaning, and the villagers could commence their work. The rewards were bountiful and gleaners could sometimes gather the equivalent of a bushel of corn, enough to make flour and bake bread for the whole family for a fortnight or more.

The legality of gleaning in Britain was first successfully challenged in 1786, when a Suffolk farmer, John Worlledge took action against

NC18961

a shoemaker from the village of Timworth, Benjamin Manning who had entered Worlledge's fields to glean barley. Two years later, in what became known as the Great Gleaning Case, the Court of Common Pleas gave judgement on a separate matter, which established the legal precedent thereafter; 'no person has at common law, the right to glean in the harvest fields'.[14] Whilst the law determined that the right to gleaning did not exist, the practise continued for many years beyond the judgement, albeit with the tacit agreement of some farmers. Hussey describes the experience of gleaners operating right up until the 1950s, when it appeared to die out completely due largely to the efficiency of new reaping and crop gathering machinery leaving little left for the village locals.

The Game Law of 1831 served to augment the isolation of the poor and push food further from the table. Where once farmers had turned a blind eye to the taking of the odd rabbit, the Game Law ushered in a covert 'war' in the countryside, one in which gamekeepers armed with lethal man-traps and other implements of destruction, were pitched against men and women driven by starvation. As pheasant and grouse were introduced to the British countryside, and woods, fields and moorland became the savannah of the tweed clad 'big game-hunters', the penalties for poaching were stiffened. Gamekeepers were given the right to make lawful arrests. The penalty for anyone caught at night with a net for poaching was transportation for seven years. In the face of such harsh punishment, poachers would often operate in large gangs, a collective response, where safety in numbers might reduce the chances of being caught. The struggle for food in the countryside was a violent one in which both poachers and gamekeepers were wounded or killed with some frequency. Poaching was so common that during the three years between 1827 and 1830, one in seven of all criminal convictions [in England] were convictions under the Game Code.[15] Poaching was by no means the preserve of the country dweller alone. The actions of urban poachers in Victorian England has attracted more recent enquiry and statistics gathered after 1858 show that poaching prosecutions in England continued to rise throughout the 1860s from around 9,000 in 1860 to just over 11,700 ten years later and peaked in

1877 at just under 12,400 cases.[16]

The overlap between the food riots of the eighteenth and nineteenth centuries and the 'poaching wars' is not insignificant, and a number of prosecutions brought about under the Game Code could rightfully be described as an out and out food fight between the poor and the state. Indeed, a number of the agrarian uprisings which occurred throughout East Anglia during the early part of the nineteenth century, were seen by the authorities as mere manifestations of the 'poaching wars', and attracted further legislation in defence of property and served to strengthen the position of the rich. The Malicious Trespass Act of 1820 introduced custodial sentences for acts of malicious injury to buildings, fences, trees and hedges.

As legislation effectively diminishing the rights of the landless poor mushroomed during this period, there was little by way of statute to alleviate their circumstances. Responsibility for administering to the poor had traditionally been one of the voluntary roles of monasteries. With the dissolution of the monasteries under Henry VIII, that responsibility gradually passed to the state, bringing with it new taxes with which to fund the relief. During the Tudor period, the Poor Laws were developed to provide a semblance of aid to 'the deserving poor' – those too weak or infirm to work. A parish-based system in which either payment of cash, or gifts of food, known commonly as 'the parish loaf' were administered to those in need. The 'undeserving poor', presumably, were left to languish in 'riotous squalor' and pilloried by the authorities in a similar way in which 'benefits scroungers' are stigmatized today.

It was the actions of food rioters, most notably the 'Swing Riots' of 1830 that gave rise to a Royal Commission in 1832, which examined the operation of the Poor Laws. Some localized attempts at alleviating the hardship of the poor had previously occurred around the country in the previous century. Driven more by a realization of the industrial inefficacies of an ailing and half-starved workforce than by a guilt-ridden embarrassment on behalf of rich landowners, employers and Justices of the Peace, the Speenhamland Act of 1795 emerged from what in effect was a meeting in a pub. In May of 1795, Charles Dundas, MP, together with the county magistrates and the Sheriff of Berkshire, met at the Pelican Inn, in Speenhamland, which is now part of Newbury in Berkshire. The meeting, in effect, fixed local wages to the price of bread and other provisions. Farmers (the majority of employers in the county) were encouraged to increase wages accordingly as the price of bread fluctuated. It transpired that the rates of pay remained largely the same, while the additional payment was provided from the parish chest. Farmers were in effect able to continue paying as little as possible for labour as the shortfall was topped up by ratepayers local to the parish. The fixing wages-to-bread prices element of the Speenhamland system was rolled out across much of the country and combined with other localized systems of poor relief. The system was seen by many in authority as fallible on two counts; firstly it tied the labourer to a handout from the parish (breeding benefit dependency in modern parlance), and secondly it presented an ever-growing bill, which had to be met by ratepayers. Further localized attempts at poor relief were to be seen in the allocation of land for use by the poor as allotments for growing their own food. Though far from widespread, as many farmers voiced concerns over the allocation of such land, this practise appeared to increase in tandem with the Poor Law reforms of 1834.

Following the series of riots which spread throughout the 'bread basket' of England, East Anglia from 1816, and then with the widespread disturbances discussed earlier known as the 'Swing Riots', which swept across southern England just over a decade later, the need for an assessment of poor relief was becoming apparent. In 1832, a Royal Commission was convened to examine the operation of the Poor Laws. Following the recommendations of the Commission, it is possible to argue that things got worse. Backed by a rhetoric which echoed the sentiments of the comments regarding the 'undeserving poor' resplendent in their riotous hovels upon the common, the Poor Law reforms of the 1830s ushered in an even more austere approach to administering relief to those in need. The Poor Law Amendment Act of 1834 marked a new definition of the ethos of provision. It established, or rather reinforced, the principles of social obligation and responsibility to the less well off, but laid that responsibility firmly at the feet of the poor, and those feet should walk them to the workhouse. These principles were to remain in place for over a century, until the creation of the welfare state following the end of the Second World War. The priorities of the new poor laws were to reduce the cost to ratepayers and to push the poor towards the free labour market which was expanding rapidly in the increasingly industrialized and urbanized areas of the country. It was clear that 'drunkards and wastrels' would now have to work for their living, rather than relying on hand outs from the local parish. Poor relief was brought into the workhouse. The building of workhouses was something that had begun towards the end of the previous century. Providing relief from within the workhouse was seen as a cheaper alternative and placed less of a strain on the parish chest. It opened up the possibilities for 'farming' the poor, as private contractors could undertake to look after a parish's poor for a fixed annual sum.[17] The labours of the poor could provide a source of income for the contractor, though the cost to the parish ratepayer would continue as the workhouse owner's annual sum would still have to be paid. In more ways than one, the welfare reforms of today can be seen to mimic, or at least share a common value with those introduced in the nineteenth century. In the past, help was only offered to those who agreed to enter the workhouse. This brought with it the notion that the state would only help those who are prepared to help themselves, and the initial act of self-help began with that step towards the workhouse. Today, welfare to work programmes, zero-hours contracts and schemes compelling Job Seeker's Allowance recipients to attend the Job Centre on a nine-to-five basis appear to echo that notion of the 'farming of the poor'. Benefits sanctions and delays are frequently given as reasons contributing to one of the most widespread food fights in modern England, to be discussed later.

The expansion of the Enclosure Acts greatly reduced individuals' capacity for 'self-sufficiency', together with the Poor Law reforms which began in the early 1830s, this effectively resulted in the 'ghettoization' of poverty. Public animosity towards this new emerging method of poor relief would later emerge in the form of a series of riots and attacks on workhouses across East Anglia and southern England. Those attacks were not solely restricted to the physical, as authors such as Charles Dickens began to describe the appalling conditions endured by the poor in popular literature of the time. The story of Oliver Twist, published in 1838, pushed poverty into the parlours of the middle and literate classes, and arguably lead to a thirst for a better understanding of poverty and its causes.

In the early part of the nineteenth century, statistical analysis of poverty was focussed rather more on the cost to the public purse, as opposed to concern with the numbers of actual people contributing to that expense. This meant that the scope of any remedial efforts was greatly limited. Figures derived from expenditure, providing the official poor law statistics at the time, appeared to show that between 1834 and 1860, poverty was in decline. The 8.5% of the population in receipt of poor relief in 1834 (an estimated 1.26 million people) had apparently dropped to 4.3% by 1860.[18] It was the work of the 'philanthropic industrialists' at the time which lead to a more robust understanding of the degree of poverty in the country. Charles Booth, who inherited his father's prosperous business and was himself a highly successful businessman, carried out an extensive survey of poverty in East London in 1887. Seebohm Rowntree (whose brother Joseph was also a renowned philanthrope) carried out research into living conditions among the poor in York in 1899. Both of these detailed studies challenged the previously held conceptions regarding the actual number of people living in poverty in England. Both studies, though in fact some ten years apart, indicated that the number of paupers among the population as a whole was closer to 30% rather than the 4.3 indicated by official statistics.

In addition to presenting a higher degree of empirical evidence of numbers, Charles Booth also came up with the concept of a 'poverty line' which provided 'an objective measure of poverty shorn of any moral or emotional assumptions'.[19] Booth determined that a family income below eighteen shillings per week would exclude that family from affording the basic nutritional elements necessary to maintain a healthy existence. The work of Booth and Rowntree paved the way for a more detailed understanding of poverty which was to inform both public opinion, and perhaps more importantly, government policy in future years. Both Booth and Rowntree were at the forefront of a tide of social and 'political' thought, which was challenging traditional notions of individualism and self-help. It appeared that the 'undeserving poor' may deserve a leg-up after all, and what's more it was perhaps in the best interests of the state to provide it. Historian Michael Rose observed in 1972 that:

> there was a growing feeling that radical cures must be found and implemented, a growing impatience with philanthropy and poor relief as mere palliatives, plasters for the sores of destitution.[20]

The 'radical cure', or at least a decent attempt at triage, was to come some decades later with the eventual emergence of the welfare state after the Second World War, though even that was arguably too short-lived to have eradicated poverty altogether.

The changing landscape over the past three centuries was ushered in through a number of stimuli. In the eighteenth and most certainly the early part of the nineteenth century, those changes were largely brought about by the ruling classes, the wealthy, and newly emerging industrialists seeking to strengthen their own positions; land grabs through enclosure, stricter laws geared towards protecting property, the use of mechanization as a means of lowering labour costs and increasing industrial output (read profit). Much of this can be seen as putting a 'squeeze' on the poor of the country, who in turn in many cases reacted to change with the best means at their disposal - riot and protest. However, over the years as the political landscape evolved, and the collective action of labourers and other less well off members of the population began to have an impact on those at the 'top', the push for change emerged from among the 'lower orders', those that would become known as the working class. As an increasingly literate and incrementally enfranchised working population began to organize itself into work unions, reformists such as William Cobbett and others began to champion their cause. With the formation of the

Labour Party as a parliamentary pressure group in 1900, it appeared that the ordinary working man (it obviously took a while longer for women to be included in the process) could at last begin to affect governmental policy through means other than social unrest.

Whilst the welfare state and universal suffrage had a direct and largely positive effect on determining the amount of food on the table of the working family, the landscape, of course, continues to change. Since the late 1970s, and the then prime minister Margaret Thatcher's denial of the existence of 'society' as a tangible political entity, the welfare state and the role of the state in tacking poverty per se, has arguably been in decline. Other factors beyond the political have started to affect the food bill of the whole nation, not just the poor. Increasing energy costs, the deregulation of the commodities market in the United States in 2000 (which opened up commodity trading to investment bankers for the first time), increasing 'unusual' weather such as droughts and floods associated with global climate change, have all had an effect on the amount of food we produce as a planet. The capacity to put food on the table has once again become an issue central to the British public, and the recent increase in the number of food banks up and down the country is surely testament to that.

The food fight in this country, it would seem, is still very much alive and kicking and as relevant today as it has ever been. The nature of that fight may have changed, as has the area in which it takes place, as well as the 'weapons' with which it is fought, but to assume that food riots are solely a thing of the past would be folly. Indeed it is remarkable that at the time of writing these words, Britain is slowly recovering from a series of floods which devastated livelihoods and business across much of southern England, and (a year later) more have recently hit the Lake District and Cumbria. Towns on the Somerset levels and parts of Oxfordshire were cut off for weeks at a time. Crops, particularly fodder crops for feeding livestock were decimated. The media broadcast the concerns of farmers and producers, who immediately began to warn of consequent rises in food prices, as the cost of importing feed from abroad and other parts of the country would have to be added to the sale of their meat.

The floods of 2014 were described across the media as 'the worst since 1766', and that of course is where my story of food worth fighting for begins.

END NOTES

1. Randall, A. *Riotous Assemblies - popular protest in Hanoverian England.*
2. Archer, J. *Social Unrest and Popular Protest in England*, p34.
3. Tate, W.E. *The English Village Community and the Enclosure Movements*, pp. 65-67.
4. Cited in Tate, W.E. *The English Village Community and the enclosure Movements*, p.23.
5. Ibid. p.50.
6. Fairlie, S. 'A Short History of Enclosure in Britain', in *The Land Magazine*, Summer 2009.
7. Ibid.
8. Cobbett, W. *Rural Rides*, p.444.
9. Cited in Tate, W.E. *The English Village Community and the Enclosure Movements*, p. 89.
10. Tate, W.E. *The English Village Community and the Enclosure Movements*, p.22.
11. Thompson, E.P. 'Rough Music Reconsidered', in *Folklore*, Vol. 103, No.1 pp 3-26.
12. Johnson, C. *An account of the Ely & Littleport Riots in 1816*, Harris & Sons, Littleport (volume reproduced by the Littleport Society www. littleportsociety.org.uk).
13. Hussey, S. 'The Changing Face of Essex Gleaning', In *The Agricultural History Review*. Vol.45 pt 2 1997.
14. King, P. 'Legal change, customary right and social conflict in the late 18th century', in *Law and History*, Spring 1992, Vol. 10, No.1.
15. Hammond & Hammond, *The Village Labourer*, p.191.
16. Osborne & Winstanley, 'Rural and Urban Poaching in Victorian England', in *Rural History*, Vol.17, No.2 p.189.
17. Higginbottom, Peter, from the website *workhouses.org.uk*
18. Rose, M.E. *The Relief of Poverty*, p.5.
19. Ibid. p.28.
20. Ibid. p.34.

CHAPTER ONE

MARCH ON THE MARKETS

THE WEST COUNTRY FOOD RIOTS OF 1766

The 1760s ushered in a decade which was particularly troublesome for the English Crown and its government. The Jacobite rebellion, during which efforts to reinstate the Stuarts to the English throne were exerted, had been thwarted not many years previously, and Bonnie Prince Charlie had long since abandoned the Isle of Skye for the warmer climes of the Mediterranean. George III had not long been on the throne, and he was no doubt keen to hang on to his seat. The country had endured the first two thirds of the Seven Years War, a 'global' conflict in the sense that the major powers at the time, Prussia, Britain, France among others, were vying for dominance both in the new world and in eastern Europe. The settlers in the American colonies were beginning to grumble about taxation without representation and were starting to have ideas of going it alone. To cap it all, the weather wasn't helping much either. 1766 saw widespread flooding, affecting grain crops as well as livestock, across Gloucestershire, Oxfordshire and Worcestershire.

The adverse weather conditions in 1766 had an almost immediate effect on the price of meat, wool and bread, further increasing the privations of the poor.[1] In his detailed work on the social conflict during the first decade of George III's reign, historian Walter Shelton, writing in 1973, identified three waves of food riots which swept across much of the West Country and southern England in 1766. The riots emerged as a response to a collection of factors, including the increases in the building of workhouses as engines and centres of poor relief in the south. The first riots, according to Shelton, were a continuation of social unrest from the previous year, while the second and third wave emerged in response to rising food prices. The typical diet of a poor country dweller at the time is described in J.C. Drummond's *The Englishman's Food* (1939). It consisted of 'good bread, cheese, pease and turnips in winter, with a little pork or other meat when they can afford it.'[2] Fresh milk was scarcely available and the actual price of meat often pushed even the cheapest cuts of pork beyond the means of a poor man's income. This description provides insight into what was clearly a very basic diet. Bread was obviously the staple of the poor man's diet, and fluctuations in the price of a loaf, or in the price of grain used for making bread would most certainly have a profound effect on the amount of food on his plate. The quality of drinking water too was a cause for concern, and home brewed ale was often seen as a safer alternative. Home brewing, however, fell into decline as the price of ingredients crept up and the increasing scarcity of fuel needed for the brewing process made the process more difficult. The rise of the country house breweries during the eighteenth century marked the onset of a nascent brewing industry as a whole and eventually sounded the death knell of all but the keenest of home brewers.

The 1750s witnessed a growth in commercial farming, which not only pushed prices up as a 'keener commercial acumen' developed among farmers, but also began to affect the structure of society as a whole. The use of turnips as a fodder crop and the introduction of clover in the crop rotation system practically eradicated the fallow year, relieving the pressure on the land through production of cereal crops. Farming was becoming more efficient, and the practises of farming families such as the Cokes of Norfolk, famed for their crop rotation practises, and sheep breeder, Robert Bakewell in Leicestershire are often cited as marking the beginnings of an agricultural revolution in England. The growth of urban areas and the need to feed armed forces engaged overseas brought lucrative contracts to large scale farmers and middlemen. New markets were developing as the Industrial Revolution began to build up a head of steam, and farmers were in a position to prosper. As a consequence, their social standing rose, putting them on a par with some of the lesser gentry of the parish. It's fair to say that new tensions were developing in this period of social change as the farmers rose to their new positions, they formed a 'buffer' between the gentry and the poor, and that buffer was to play a role, arguably contributing to the spread of food riots over many counties. Much of the anger of food rioters at this time was directed at farmers and middlemen. Initially, the gentry were unaffected by the disturbances, but that was to change. In some areas of the country, the gentry had encouraged the poor to regulate markets themselves, a practise that was to get a little out of hand.

Market regulation was not uncommon at the time. Members of the public would gather at markets and fix the prices of bread and corn themselves. Such 'committees' would often dictate to merchants the 'fair price' of goods for sale. By today's standards, this approach to the weekly shop takes some explaining, as apart from haggling with a market stall holder seeking to make a final sale as he packs away for the day, we rarely get to influence the price of our shopping basket in such a direct manner. During the middle of the eighteenth century, things were a little different. Markets in the eighteenth century served in a way, as 'political arenas', a venue where a dialogue could take place, which would hopefully produce a mutually satisfactory outcome. They were influenced by a dialogue between vendors and customers, which was often sanctioned by the local authorities. The customers were informed by prices and practices from recent trading, and vendors responded to this. It wasn't the 'market' that set prices, that was done by people negotiating within the market place. Things, however, were beginning to change, and change rather rapidly, particularly as widespread commercial farming was on the increase. Corn merchants (sometimes larger scale land-owning farmers themselves, as well as middle men too) at the time, were beginning to see the benefits of improved transport systems; better roads, new canal and river networks were making the transportation of corn a lot easier. The market for farm produce was expanding as the Industrial Revolution gathered pace. The existing corn laws, geared towards maintaining a high price, worked largely to the benefit of the larger landowners and producers and the period saw a boom in 'middlemen' stepping in to facilitate the movement of grain to and between markets, as well as for export.

By the autumn of 1766, however, a series of poor harvests, exacerbated by unusually inclement weather, had reduced the availability of fodder crops, thus pushing up the price of meat as well as that of grain. Poor harvests across Europe meant there was already a market for English grain abroad, though in times of scarcity, people were less than happy to see shipments of grain being prepared for export. In January 1766, a crowd of some 600 people gathered at Winchester, threatening to sink corn barges destined for export abroad.[3] A great deal of anger was directed towards the 'middlemen' as they were seen as a legitimate target, and were often perceived as dishonest since some were given to forestalling (withholding stocks of food in order to gain a better price at market), or adulterating food and offering up short measures. 'The miller's thumb', which throughout most of my life I took to describe a particular species of small freshwater fish with an over-size head, was also a reference to a surreptitious device employed by less than scrupulous millers. In weighing out flour for customers, some of the less honest millers were given to tipping the scales with a deft press of the thumb, as a means of adjusting the transaction in their favour. Butchers too occasionally gained a reputation as employing deception in their methods of increasing the takings of the till by bulking out sausages with rusk as an example. In times of food shortage such as was prevalent in 1766, the temptation on behalf of traders to eek out their wares and increase their profits must have been particularly strong and difficult to resist.

The practise of food adulteration was by no means a new phenomenon at the time, and could indeed often have a far more harmful effect on the customer than the mere offering of short measures. Since 1266, and for more than 500 years following, the price and quality of bread and ale were controlled by the system of Assizes.[4] The system was administered by local inspectors, and offences dealt with in regularly held courts, or Assizes. Offenders were subject to hefty fines or pillory in public. Though there is little evidence to suggest that food adulteration might have been a widespread practise during the early part of the eighteenth century, millers, grain merchants, brewers and other food producers were not averse to adding small quantities of ground alum to flour, adding sugar to beer to mask the effects of dilution, or bulking out a load of grain with the odd fistful of tiny pebbles. Enforcement of the system of bread Assizes was beginning to wane by the mid 1700s. Social historian, John Burnett, has observed, however, that by the closing decades of this century, the quality of many foods was becoming more and more suspect. Largely as a result of increasing urbanization, and the migration of people from the countryside to the rapidly growing towns, the practice of food adulteration was becoming a lucrative business. The risks of being exposed as a dodgy dealer were greatly reduced while operating in a town or city, rather than a smaller community where word could get around more easily. It wasn't until the nineteenth century that the issue of food adulteration was more thoroughly researched, and the potentially murderous consequences of tampering with food were exposed. The first Food Adulteration Act was not passed until 1860.

In an atmosphere of uncertainty, brought on by a series of bad harvests, an enduring war abroad, exceptional flooding and growing doubts about the integrity of what little food there was available to the poor in the English countryside, the food riots of 1766 kicked off with a trip to the market. In actual fact, it was several trips by large numbers of hungry and angry people, to several markets across the south west of England that ushered in a series of food riots which would stretch the resources of law and order to breaking point.

Historian John Bohstedt has identified over 160 food riots occurring in the Midlands and across southern England during 1766.[5] Fuelled and reassured by a strong sense of communal action, people took it upon themselves to fix prices which they and others could afford. Grain seized from merchants and millers was brought to the market and distributed at an affordable price. In many cases, the carts and sacks used for transporting the grain were returned to the rightful owners, together with the revenue raised from the sale. This was not robbery, rather a tool by which the rioters could exhort some form of control over prices. Acts of seizure and distribution were described as riots by the aggrieved merchants and the authorities tasked with dealing with them. Shelton has observed that as many magistrates failed to suppress the initial disorders, they were seen to sanction the acts of the rioters. They faced a truly difficult task, as John Bohstedt puts it:

> magistrates wheedled, bargained with and exhorted cornmasters, farmers and rioters, not simply to parley, but more often to negotiate in action and reaction through social turbulence, just as a boatman negotiates rapids with a skill as much dance as design.[6]

Magistrates' efforts at balancing force with remedy within their communities, may explain the initial rapid spread of riots and disturbances. In their 'wheedling', magistrates clearly alluded to a certain legitimacy in the rioter's complaint and actions. The gentry and governments, on the other hand, were initially protected by the 'buffer' provided by the farmers, corn masters and middlemen, and so in many cases were inclined to tolerate the riots as a factor of the 'market'. Bohstedt has described this as 'the politics of provisions', an interactive struggle for food between the people and their rulers. Indeed it appears that in some cases, the gentry were happy to further, and even direct rioters' attentions to the machinations of the middlemen. This, however, was soon to change and the 'free market', that is to say a market free of intervention from over exuberant customers seeking to fix their own prices, would triumph as food riots were suppressed and participants dealt with by the forces of law and order.

The Riot Act was read so many times in 1766, it must have made it on to the bestseller list for that year. From Cornwall to the Midlands and beyond, rioters were engaged in direct action. Markets in Truro, Exeter, Bath, Newbury, Lechlade, Stroud, Worcester, Kidderminster and many other towns were subject to scenes of tumult and presumably joy as food was, albeit without the consent of the owners, distributed at affordable prices among those least well off. Thompson describes a powerful motif, which was often used to signify the beginning of a crowd action; in many cases, a loaf of bread was raised on a stick, around which would gather a crowd of protestors intent of interfering at the market place.[7] In Gloucestershire, the riots began in Stroud on Friday 12th September. The High Sheriff of the county, William Dallaway, described the unfolding events. His opening description invokes the image of a 'ran tan', a call for 'rough music', 'On Friday last, a mob was raised in these parts by the blowing of horns'.[8] Dallaway goes on to say that the mob comprised 'the lowest of the population, weavers, mechanics, labourers and prentice boys'. The rioters marched on Stroud market where according to Dallaway, they 'pilfered the market peoples' commodities and [horror of all horrors] insulted the bakers'. Similar events took place a week or so later at Cirencester market. Crowds of up to 1,500 strong gathered, again under flags and the call of hunting horns. Vast quantities of foodstuffs were seized and sold at affordable prices. Wheat was sold at five shillings a bushel and cheese for two or two and a half pennies per pound in weight.[9] The fact that seized grain and other foodstuffs was distributed and sold at market by the rioters, and in many cases, sacks and carts returned to their owners, tends to suggest a degree of 'honest thuggery' among those involved. It must have made it difficult for the authorities at the time to deal with the riots effectively. The intentions of those seizing stocks of grain were to the benefit of the many, and in the eyes of those customers, must have been seen as a legitimate (morally at least) course of action, and to an extent, this belief was propped up by the manner in which the authorities initially responded. Shelton remarks that:

'a crucial feature of the hunger riots of 1766 was the initial encouragement given to the mobs by the ruling orders in the countryside. In an age when prompt action by the local authorities invariably snuffed out riots before they became a real social threat, the restraint of the majority of the gentry-magistrates towards riotous mobs was extraordinary and tantamount to sanction.'[10]

This sentiment is reflected in an 'advertisement to the poor' which appeared in East Anglia at the time:[11]

To the Poor

The Magistrates pity you, and you may be assured they will use every endeavour to obtain PLENTY and CHEAPNESS of PROVISIONS.

The greater quantity which is brought to the market, the more plentiful and cheaper it must be.

But if the Country are driven out, and not suffered to come In peace, there can be neither plenty nor cheapness.

Rioting will stop the provisions coming to market, and will increase the present Distress of the Poor, and, at the same time, will make it impossible for the Magistrates to do anything to serve them.

In compassion to your distress the Magistrates would not read the proclamation [the Riot Act], they wish to avoid it.

For God's sake do not drive things to extremities: The Magistrates are sworn to keep the peace, and in all events they must do their duty.

This 'advertisement' appears to be appealing to the better nature of the rioters, yet seemingly allows them to have their 'sales' in the market place. It is almost as if they are encouraging participants to bring more provisions to the market for distribution, while fully realizing the 'distresses' under which the poor exist. Regardless of the imploring of the magistrates for calm, things were getting steadily more raucous to say the least. Further proclamations by the authorities were made which, while appearing to recognize some of the concerns of the rioters, also began to lay more responsibility at their feet. A proclamation in the

Leicester and Nottingham Journal, 4 October 1766 sets out quite clearly the requirement for rioters to amend their behaviour.

> The Consequences of your late Riots are Terrible: Thousands of you have been guilty of Felony; many already imprison'd, the Magistrates will do their Duty; what must be the Event to yourselves; without this necessary exertion of their Power you'll be all Starv'd; Think before its too late. Every Thing that can be thought of has been done for your Benefit. The Exportation of Wheat is at an End; the Distillery is stopp'd; the Laws against Regrating and Forestalling are order'd to be put in Execution; Farmers have been requir'd to bring Provisions to Market. And nothing but your own Indiscretion can prevent your reaping the Benefit.[12]

These were riots born of hunger, and whilst a degree of 'fair play' among the rioters was clearly present in the distribution of grain and the returning of property, there were obviously scenes of physical violence in the market place. According to historian Adrian Randall however, the rioters were not the violent desperadoes they were often seen as being. Whilst the mob may have appeared very threatening, with its noise, numbers and threats, much of this was part of the 'theatre of riot', in which horns, flags and ceremonial destruction of 'immoral' property such as bunting mills played a role. They were a crowd made up of labourers and skilled and semi skilled artisans, and they were prepared to travel some distance to get their point across. Accounts in newspapers from the time, however, appear to challenge the beneficent integrity of the rioters, and sadly in not every case were the proceeds of a forced sale returned to the owner.

Dated 28th September 1766, an account from *The Bath Chronicle & Weekly Gazette* describes events in the Midlands:

> There was great rioting here on Friday last, by the colliers from the neighbouring pits and the townspeople, who readily joined them. They took a wagonload of cheese out of one of the storehouses to the market cross and began to sell it by weight, but that was very

soon over, so they sold large cheeses for 1s 6d and 1s per cheese, but that also soon ceased, for the mob took it without money or price: they carried a cartload of cheese away and only carried the owner three shillings for it. It was all deposed of at the open cross. There were more wagonloads of wheat at the cross on that day than ever I saw at any one time before, and oats also for I gave 10s for one bag of Poland oats.

These contemporary reports help build a picture of the goings-on and were typical of similar events throughout the west of England. E.P. Thompson cites an account of lace workers seizing corn and bearing it to market for sale, returning the proceeds as well as the sacks to the farmers.[13] Labourers, colliers, bargemen, skilled craftsmen and other ordinary working people who suddenly found that they could no longer feed their families, took to the streets and market places in a bid to address their situation. Expropriation of food was a common form of riot and it wasn't always the case that the victuals were brought to market for distribution. Examples of such actions were recorded in local newspapers and journals at the time. The splendidly named, 'Valentine Yarnspinner', of the Nottingham Radical History Group, 'People's Histreh', describes events in the Midlands as recorded by the *Leicester and Nottingham Journal* in October of 1766.

The passage explains how expropriations continued in Leicester, despite a large military presence there and efforts on behalf of the authorities to organize a controlled sale at reduced prices.

Rioting had erupted after a load of cheese was stopped from being carted out of town. The cheese on the wagon was distributed 'whole before the Magistrates received any Information of these proceedings'. Afterwards the rioting quickly spread through town despite a large troop of infantry having been mobilised almost instantly. A large amount of cheese, which had been stashed in a pub, was distributed and a number of stores and warehouses searched. In the evening, groups of rioters began systematically to search wagons going in and out of the town in order to discover further provisions, and were able to expropriate further commodities before the military could intervene.[14]

Riot, however, was not restricted to the market place alone. In many cases, the resentment towards perceived adulterers of food and suspected forestallers was vented in a more violent form. Large numbers of bolting mills, or bunting mills, buildings where flour was sifted and graded, were ransacked and destroyed by rioters amid accusations of foul play in the bunting mill. In destroying the bunting mills, rioters were also actively seeking to disrupt the export of grain, presumably with the intention of ensuring more provisions remain in the country for domestic use. In the early part of 1766, the authorities seemed willing to tolerate the disturbances, particularly as anger was directed towards the growing body of middlemen as opposed to the large land owning gentry. There is an argument to be made which states that while the mobs were venting their anger and carrying out attacks on middlemen and forestallers, the gentry were little affected and less inclined to severe action. There was a view that the occurrence of riots provided a convenient safety valve through which the pressures of privation among the poor could be let off. It could be argued that the fact that rioters were targeting specific individuals, the 'evil forestaller' or the 'greedy miller' for example, was to the benefit of the authorities at the time. With the anger of the crowd focussed on individuals, rather than the broader economic system, the status quo was for the time being at least unaffected. But as the scale and scope of the riots began to spread, a corresponding fear among the landed gentry and establishment grew, particularly as they witnessed increasing violence and damage towards buildings and property. Accordingly a perceived threat to the buildings on country estates was soon spreading among the establishment. It was only at this point that the authorities sought to quell the riots in their entirety. Efforts to reduce the number of riots breaking out, particularly around the centres of transport, were made by banning the export of corn. In 1766 an embargo on corn exports was in place for almost six months in the year, marking what looked like a clear 'win' for the rioters. Proclamations such as those cited above, which promised to tackle the wrong-doings of forestallers, were made by magistrates. A ban on the distillation of grain based alcohol and the starch making industry (both of which served to divert scarce crops from the table) was introduced in September of 1766. The carrot was offered and the stick was soon to follow.

The uniform nature of the spreading riots, first manifesting as seizures and forced sales at market crosses, and then out and out expropriation and free distribution of foodstuffs, spreading to more violent attacks on middlemen and the bunting mills as well as mill owners themselves, and in some cases breweries, was now a cause for concern among the upper levels of society. Increasing numbers of returning veterans from the Seven Years War among the rioters appeared to bring with them a form of 'discipline' to the riots. Former soldiers were in a position to use their military knowledge and experience to counter attempts by local militia to settle disturbances. Shelton describes events in Warwickshire, where a 'mob of 1,000 divided into gangs of 300 or 400 which simultaneously visited several neighbouring market towns'.[15] Such action appears to suggest a degree of military experience in co-ordinating action across a large area in order to weaken any opposition. The growth of the riots across south western England were rapidly fuelling fears among the establishment of an all out revolution.

Indeed, fear of a revolution along the lines of that building across the English Channel led the establishment and authorities at the time to take the food riots very seriously indeed. Increasingly, the army was called in to deal with disturbances. Reliance on the use of volunteer militias declined, as militia men were often drawn from among communities they were sent to suppress. By utilizing the services of the regular professional army, local authorities were relieved of the inconvenience of any 'local sympathies' and were accordingly able to deal with tumult and uprising in an altogether more brutal manner. In short, the initially empathetic approach taken by local magistrates seeking to deal with disturbances through negotiation and appeasement, was replaced with a force more akin to that used by the authorities in the twentieth century when dealing with the miners strike or the 'Peace Convoy' – new age travellers in the 1980s. By November, the vast majority of riots had been effectively dealt with. Participants were arrested en-masse and a travelling special commission was convened to try those who had been caught. The commission moved from county to county passing sentence on hundreds of rioters. Examples were made and those convicted were either hung, transported or drafted into service in the navy. The impact of this last sentence would presumably have had a devastating effect on those who had chosen seamanship as a profession, putting service in said institution on a par with capital punishment or transportation. Regardless, by December 1766, the food riots which had swept much of south western England had been quashed. In Gloucester alone, 96 prisoners appeared before the special commission. Nine were sentenced to death, of which three, Stephen Cratchley, Joseph Wildery and Aaron Prims were hanged at Gloucester in January 1767. The death sentence was commuted to transportation for the remaining six.

One of the key points of interest about the food riots of 1766 is the initial interaction (or possibly lack of it) between the landed gentry and the poor who were actually engaged in riot. Some historians suggest that by directing rioters' attention to the alleged malpractices of middle men, the gentry were in effect suggesting, or seeking to give the impression that the food shortages and soaring prices were an 'artificial' phenomenon in the control of avaricious businessmen and thus indirectly the central authorities played an important role in the diversion of the poor towards specific targets.[16] This clearly served to divert the frustrations and actions of the crowd away from the establishment. Whilst it was certainly a bout of sustained inclement weather in the early part of the year which gave rise to food shortages and corresponding price hikes, the fact that the gentry played a part in propagating an 'artificial' element to the reason behind soaring food prices certainly begs the question as to why. Personally, I see the answer wrapped in the fear of revolution. Historian Adrian Randall suggests there was actually little prospect of a revolution at the time, as the food rioters had no conception of a social order other than that in which they lived. I'm not so sure I agree with him. Randall maintains that the lack of a coherent view, on behalf of the rioters, of an alternative structure of power, means that revolution was never on the minds of the rioters. There may even be further evidence for Randall's claims, in that the demands of the rioters in the market places never went beyond a call for food at fair prices. There were no calls for higher wages or other such demands that may have improved the lot of 'the lowest of the population'. There were no overt political demands. These were to come at a later date as the Industrial Revolution began to shape society in the coming century. I believe that those with a lot more to lose than a mere barn full of corn, or milling equipment which could easily be replaced once destroyed, were indeed frightenend of what might emerge from the riots. By persuading rioters to focus on individuals, rather than the prevailing social and economic system, I believe that the landed gentry were protecting their own positions and, perhaps unwittingly, did indeed avert a revolution. To assume that a lack of a coherent vision of a political alternative precludes any desire for revolution flies in the face of what we have witnessed in the twenty-first century, particularly with the advent of the 'Arab spring'. In calling for change, as opposed to out and out revolution, crowd action can topple governments. I think that the authorities at the time realized this and acted shrewdly, managing by the skin of their teeth to hang on to positions of privilege without having to make many concessions at all. The notion of the market place as a 'political arena' in this case, appears to ring true, it's just that the discourse which took place over much of southern England in 1766 appears to have had a greater effect on the machinations of the market itself rather than on any 'broadening' in a political sense.

As the authorities began to clamp down more heavily on the crowds, and food rioters were captured, charged and sentenced, it is possible to argue that markets across the country were 'freed', that is to say, freed from public intervention. Bohstedt notes in his introduction to *The Politics of Provision* (2010), that 'Free markets were ultimately freed, not simply from state regulation, but also from crowds' direct action'.[17] Old traditions and practices of price setting in the market place were no longer tolerated after this period. The tumult in the market place eventually came to be seen by the authorities, not as a 'pressure valve' through which political frustration might be vented, but as a threat to their own existence. The ruling classes were awakened by their own complacency. Their arrogance towards the lower classes had led to them accepting a degree of tumult and affray, as 'the poor fought it out among themselves', but now there was clearly more at risk. The authorities of law and order were brought in to protect the market. Prices were from now on to be determined by the market alone, and one of the roles of the authorities was to ensure that this new 'free market' could operate without let or hindrance from frustrated customers.

END NOTES

1. Shelton, W. *English Hunger and Industrial Disorders*, p.31.
2. Cited in Drummond, J.C. *The Englishman's Food*, p.208.
3. Bohstedt, J. 'A Census of Riots' in *Politics of Provisions*, appendix.
4. Burnett, J. *Plenty & Want*, p.101.
5. Bohstedt, J. *The Politics of Provisions*, appendix.
6. Ibid. p.2.
7. Thompson, E.P. *The Making of the English Working Class*, p.70.
8. Cited in Randall, A. *The Gloucester Food Riots of 1766.*
9. Ibid.
10. Shelton, W. *English Hunger and Industrial Disorders,* p.95.
11. Cited in Shelton, W. *English Hunger and Industrial Disorders,* p.98 by Courtesy of the Norfolk and Norwich Record office.
12. Cited in 'Damn his Charity, we'll have the Cheese for nought! Nottingham's Great Cheese Riot & other 1766 Food Riots' - a pamphlet produced by Peoples Histreh, Nottingham's Radical History Group. www. peopleshistreh.wordpress.com
13. Thompson, E.P. *The Making of the English Working Class.*
14. Cited in 'Damn his Charity, we'll have the Cheese for nought! Nottingham's Great Cheese Riot & other 1766 Food Riots' - a pamphlet produced by Peoples Histreh, Nottingham's Radical History Group. www. peopleshistreh.wordpress.com
15. Shelton, W. *English Hunger and Industrial Disorders*, p.125
16. Ibid. p.121
17. Bohstedt. J, *The Politics of Provisions.*

CHAPTER TWO

AGAINST THE GRAIN

The Ely and Littleport 'Bread and Beer' Riots of 1816

The food of the agricultural labourer depended upon his general standard of living, and that standard depended, in turn, on the state of the agricultural economy of which he was a part. In good times he might fare not too badly, in bad ones he was the first to suffer, and the difficulty was that agricultural prosperity was determined by a number of external factors – the demand for farm produce, the movement of prices, the extent of foreign competition – over which he had no influence. Uneducated and unenfranchised, immobilised by poverty and the poor laws, the labourer was peculiarly exposed to the vicissitudes of trade and the seasons, and in no real sense the master of his own destiny.[1]

Towards the end of the eighteenth century, and into the early nineteenth century, a number of factors came about which must have amplified the labourer's sense of lack of control over his own destiny. Key to those factors was the role and the notion of the new emerging free market. In 1775, Scottish economist and philosopher, Adam Smith, published his ground-breaking fundamental work on economics, *Wealth of Nations*. In it, Smith argued that by interfering with the market, through imposing controls, taxes and tariffs, governments made their people poorer, rather than richer. Smith's ideas were to have an almost immediate and lasting effect on governments of the time, and change was slowly instigated, through his understanding of the plight of the village labourer. However, it would not be easy. With the food riots of the previous century having led to a freeing of the markets from direct public intervention, coupled with Adam Smith's notions of freeing the market from government intervention, the hungry labourer faced a mighty struggle.

The struggle for land in East Anglia, often referred to as 'the bread basket of England', arguably dates back as far as the sixteenth century. In a sense, it was as much a political issue as it was a physical endeavour, as the first successful attempts at draining the fens coincided with the early Acts of Enclosure. Land was wrested not only from the clutches of the encroaching sea, but also from the reach of the common man, leaving behind a landless cohort of men whose only means of earned income would be through attempting to sell their labour.

In the face of a number of years of bad harvests, and the state of war with France bringing concerns over food production, the Board of Agriculture was established in 1793. The Board of Agriculture was essentially a private affair, but one bolstered with considerable government grants to cover its expenses. It very quickly began to espouse the merits of enclosure as a means of improving the 'efficiency' of the land. The General Enclosure Act of 1801 was soon to follow, and marked a not insignificant increase in the amount of common land being taken into private possession.

> In almost every enclosure the poorer sections of the community
> suffered either directly or indirectly. Small owners often found
> the cost of fencing, hedging and ditching prohibitive and had

no alternative but to sell their land and become wage labourers. Arthur Young [a writer on agriculture and economics d.1820] likened the process to stealing a man's handkerchief and then employing him to embroider the new owner's initials on it.[2]

The war with France brought with it a rise in prices. Napoleon's tactics of employing a 'continental system' in an attempt to blockade trade between Britain and countries loyal to France, were a response to the British blockade of the French coast. Both the British and the French were in effect using food as a weapon of war, a concept which comes in to play in a later chapter. This 'economic warfare', augmented by a succession of poor harvests across Europe, amounted to a boon for farmers and producers, but a hardening of times for the poor. The end of the Napoleonic Wars in 1815 saw a fall in the price of grain and also brought with it a number of further strains on the lot of the agricultural labourer, namely falling wages. The Corn Law of 1815 was introduced to prop up the price of corn, ensuring that all domestic stocks of corn were sold before imported corn was allowed to find its way to market. The plight of the labourer was exacerbated by a marked decrease in the amount of arable land that was worked in the immediate aftermath of the war, as well as a rapid demobilization of troops, which saw many ex-servicemen returning to their towns and villages in the countryside, contributing to a glut in available labour in the rural areas of the country. In 1813, wheat sold at 120s. a quarter; in 1815 it stood at 76s. and by 1822 it had fallen to 53s.[3] The fall in wheat prices should by accounts have benefitted the poor labourers, but a peculiar manifestation of the Poor Laws designed to protect the most vulnerable meant that the amount of relief a family might receive from the local parish was directly linked to the price of bread, as well as the number of children in the family. The 'bread scale' or 'Speenhamland' system had been brought to bear by a number of magistrates meeting in a pub, the Pelican Inn in Speenhamland in Berkshire in 1795. Amid soaring food prices at the time, local notables had sought to avert dissent among the poor by supplementing inadequate wages with an allowance from the local parish. The Speenhamland system effectively allowed farmers to pay less than a living wage and thus rendered the recipient of welfare entirely dependent upon the coffers of the local parish.

The poor of East Anglia, much like those in the rest of the country, survived on a basic diet of bread and potatoes as staples, supplemented with small amounts of tea, cheese, bacon and butter. Lacking the wherewithal to purchase a more varied diet, many labourers would rely on poaching as a means of bringing fresh meat to the table. As if to rub salt in a wound (not that the poor labourer could afford to buy salt), the existing game laws further broadened the gap between landowner and wage labourer. With penalties of death or transportation for those caught poaching, and deadly iron spiked mantraps deployed to deter others who might be considering such a career move, a 'poaching war' between the gentry and the common man was fought all over the country. The rapid expansion of the number of enclosures made during the war years (around 1,400 enclosure acts were passed between 1790 and 1810)[4] must have had a considerable impact on the 'range' of the poacher. Such a significant reduction in the amount of common land, and a corresponding expansion of newly enclosed 'private property', probably made it easier for a gamekeeper to catch a poacher, than it was for a poacher to catch a hare.

The relationship between the poaching gangs and the riots which were to break out in 1816 across East Anglia, is emphasized by historian A.J. Peacock and gives an insight into not only the motives (in part at least) of the rioters, but also perhaps their means of communication. As moves to tighten laws against poaching were introduced, resistance to arrest became more violent amongst those caught. One of the avowed aims of the Downham rioters in May was to liberate the poachers recently imprisoned in the local gaol.[5] That poachers worked in gangs, presumably as a means of protection as well as improving the efficiency of the 'hunt', is well established. It is also clear that agricultural labourers in the area were also employed in gangs as they sold their labour to local farmers and landowners. The potential for a degree of overlap in both 'professions' in a such a relatively small rural area is surely not beyond the realms of possibility. Communication among and between the men working as colleagues in the fields by day, and those who sought to put food on the table at home 'working' under the dark of night must have been in free flow. It is easy to see that as dissent grew and as riot broke out, word was spread across the fens very quickly.

Many labourers were also members of 'Benefit Clubs' or so called friendly societies, which were established as a means of support for their members. A small, regular donation from members would yield a degree of financial support in hard times, and a higher degree of camaraderie and companionship year round. These societies were often at the time viewed by local magistrates and clergymen (often one and the same) as potentially seditious bodies. The clubs were given to meet regularly in public houses, where the obvious consumption of beer might assist in the inflammation of disputes.

The food, or bread, riots that broke out across East Anglia in April and May of 1816, spread rapidly among a number of towns and villages in close proximity; Brandon, Downham Market, Norwich, Bury St Edmunds, Ely and Littleport all witnessed scenes of violence and tumult. The riots can be seen as a direct response to poverty, hunger and lack of employment as the prices of bread and flour began to rise in the spring of 1816. It is a common misconception that the riots were started solely by disgruntled unemployed ex-soldiers returning from the Napoleonic Wars. Whilst is true that the return of ex-servicemen to the area clearly added to the numbers of those finding themselves without work, as had occurred in the previous century at the end of the seven years war, Peacock demonstrates that the majority of rioters did not have a military background, and were mainly made up of agricultural labourers.[6] These riots were born of hunger, rather than through the dissatisfaction of returning war heroes.

One of the earliest riots took place in the parish of Gosbeck in Suffolk, where a crowd of around twenty men took to breaking farm machinery, which was seen as coming to replace the work of manual labours and contributing to the extensive rise of unemployment. Other events of a similar nature broke out in the area, but by the time of the riots in Downham, and later Ely and Littleport, the participating labourers began to declare reasons other than the threat from mechanization for their actions. As mentioned, one of the aims of the Downham rioters was to free the poachers imprisoned there. A call common to almost all of the riots which occurred throughout East Anglia in 1816 was that of 'Bread or Blood'. Rioters carried the motif on placards and it served to illustrate the desperate position many of those participating had found themselves in. Another rallying call to action was the sign of a loaf on a stick held high above a gathering crowd. Of all the riots, those at Ely and Littleport, were perhaps the most tumultuous. Some eighty people were charged for various offences and appeared before Justices; Burrough, Abbott and Christian at the special Assizes convened in the courts at Ely to deal with those who took part.

The men of the Littleport 'Benefit Club' met at The Globe public house on the evening of 22 May, where most likely over a beer or two they might have discussed the recent disturbances in nearby towns and villages; it would surely have been difficult not to. Rioters at nearby Downham Market had succeeded, initially at least, in pressing promises of cheaper bread and increased relief from the parish from local magistrates. That these promises were never kept, and prices of bread continued to rise, more than likely caused anger and upset further afield.

Fired-up with ale, it appears that the Littleport labourers decided to pay a visit to the local vicar and magistrate, a Rev John Vachell. Vachell agreed to meet with the crowd and to speak with a local (and deeply unpopular) farmer, Mr Henry Martin. As in other areas, the crowd were promised two shillings a day parish relief, and flour at two shillings sixpence per stone. Despite this apparent conciliatory approach from the local magistrate, and perhaps in recognition of the fact that Vachell's promises were highly unlikely to come to fruition, others in the crowd took to rioting, robbery and extorting money from local shopkeepers and landlords. The assembly appears to have moved from house to shop to house, threatening owners and helping themselves to cash and valuables. According to Peacock,[7] the labourers began to organize themselves and arrived at the house of a Rayner Brassett, a local baker and flour dealer. The unfortunate Brassett was allocated the impromptu role of accountant for the evening's takings and ordered to note the value of the booty so far collected. A total of £25 was left in the care of Mrs Brassett, and the baker and his wife were assured that the crowd would be back the following day to collect their takings.

The crowd moved on in search of Henry Martin who had earlier made promises in a bid to calm the rising mood. Martin lived with his grandmother, a shopkeeper named Mrs Rebecca Waddelow. Though Martin managed to escape the angry crowd, his granny was forced to part with a deal of cash and most of the contents of her shop, as the crowd cleared the place of food and clothing. One account records the misfortune of an un-named rioter who found what he thought was a bag of sugar; on tearing the packet open and pouring the contents into his mouth, he soon found his booty to be mustard and 'at once rushed to a pail of beer and washed his mouth out'.[8] The riot went on well into the evening and ended up back at the Reverend Vachell's house, with the labourers demanding money and beer from the clergyman. Not happy with the £2 and barrel of beer supplied, the mob proceeded to smash up the vicar's house and remove anything of value.

Plans were made for a march on Ely the next day, as the crowd reassembled at the Globe pub, for what was presumably a rather lively 'lock-in'! Ahead of the morrow's march, the crowd sought to arm themselves with firearms, shot and powder. An account in the *Cambridge Chronicle* dated 7 June 1816 details rioters armed with 'guns, pitchforks, bludgeons and large fowling guns'. The following day a cart was found and the large fowling gun mounted up front. With what must have looked like some sort of primitive horse-drawn armoured car, bristling with guns and other weapons, the mob set off for Ely in the early hours of the following morning with labourer George Crow at the reins.

Rev William Metcalfe, an Ely magistrate, met the Littleport men on the outskirts of town. Metcalfe tried unsuccessfully to persuade the approaching procession to turn around. A crowd of some 500 persons gathered in the market place at Ely, where Metcalfe and a group of other magistrates asked the armed group what they wanted. The familiar reply of 'two shillings from the parish, and flour at two shillings sixpence' was embellished by a rather optimistic Richard Rutter, who added a demand for beer at tuppence a pint! The rioters must have thought that they were in a commanding position, as a delegation was invited to join with the magistrates in the White Hart Inn, where a declaration was drawn up to the effect that; each family shall receive two shillings per head per week when flour is half a crown a stone, and that allowance shall be raised in proportion when the price of flour rises. The proclamation also stated that the price of labour be set at two shillings per day and that wages were to be paid in full by the hiring farmer.

It must have appeared to the Littleport labourers that their demands and grievances were seen by the magistrates as both legitimate, and worthy of commitment. The fact that these concessions were gained under threat of violence, and would not be honoured appeared to escape the labourers' minds as the majority of them returned to Littleport, and more specifically to The Globe public house. The baker, Rayner Brassett, was called upon to divvy up the takings from the previous days rioting and pay for beer for the celebrating crowd. Such was the extent of the party, Brassett was obliged to distribute the ill gotten gains of the previous night among the landlords of The Crown, The George and The Turk's Head. Later, on turning Crown Witness, Brassett was to claim that he paid for the evening's carousing from his own pocket, rather than touch the ill gotten 'kitty' of the rioters.

Some of the Littleport labourers remained in Ely and were joined by men from Downham, and together with a number of women, continued rioting and demanding money from shopkeepers and beer from publicans, 'the rest of Thursday was given over to rioting and drinking in Ely, the publicans being forced to supply food and drink'.[9] By now, magistrates had sent for military assistance from the First Royal Dragoon Guards, stationed in Bury St Edmunds. The Ely magistrates had also begun to swear-in special constables from among the local tradesmen. Initially, only a small body of men could be spared for deployment. Some sixteen Dragoons arrived at Ely, where the commanding officer joked, having served at Waterloo; they were now fighting the 'battle of Hullabaloo'. A number of prisoners were taken by the Ely authorities, and plans were made for a march on Littleport the following day.

A number of volunteers from the Royston Troop of Yeoman Cavalry joined the Dragoons as they marched towards Littleport. The majority of the rioters were to be found in the George and Dragon pub. Apart from barricading the windows, and a shot fired from the pub which wounded one of the soldiers, the Littleport men put up little resistance, and were eventually dragged outside by the militia. At this point, the first fatality of the riots occurred as the unfortunate Thomas Sindall sought to make an escape. Ignoring a command to stop, Sindall was shot in the head by one of the soldiers. He died on the spot.

A total of eighty arrests were made, and some men went into hiding only to be betrayed by their hosts, as the reward for information leading to arrests was set at £5. Others made their escape to London; a William Gotobed managed to lie low in the capital for seven years before returning to Littleport under a pardon. Those arrested were returned to Ely. Some fifty-four people, including two women, were committed for trial either for rioting or for offences connected with the riots. The youngest was a John Burrage, aged only thirteen years, and the oldest was a Mark Benton, aged sixty. Of the two women arrested, only Sarah Hobbs stood trial.

A special commission was appointed for the trial, which began on Monday 17 June 1816. Three judges were appointed to try the accused, James Burrough, Charles Abbott and Edward Christian (whose mutinous brother, Fletcher, seized the HMS Bounty from Captain Bligh in 1789). From the outset it was clear that the government intended that the trial and its outcome be a warning to other potential rioters. In his opening address, Abbott claimed that the 'natural progress of triumphant insurrection is to increase in fury and to grow larger in its demands'. He refuted the claims of the defendants stating that 'the pretence of these lawless disturbances seems to have been the necessity of an advance in the wages of husbandry, but the circumstances of some among the offenders do not correspond with the supposition of such an object'. Much was made during the hearings of claims that some of the rioters owned, or had regular access to land, and that their relative poverty was not the cause of the disturbances, rather a mere grievance. Abbott seemingly acknowledged the tough conditions under which the defendants lived, 'It happened that the hardships necessarily incident to a state of poverty were aggravated by the peculiarity of the seasons', but was adamant that the riots were born of a 'settled hostility against the higher orders of society'.

The warning to other would be rioters is clear when he went on to say:

> It is fit however that I should make one observation which is, that there are many offences committed by large assemblies of men, in which guilt is not confined to the individual whose hand executed the felonious act. All those are present at its commission, who favour it with their approbation and concurrence, or who aid and encourage by their voice or action, are involved in the same legal culpability.[10]

Basically, if you were there among the crowd, even as a mere observer, you were just as guilty as the worst of them. Abbott closed his speech stating that it is of the highest importance to peace and safety throughout the land, that those who hear the account of the proceedings are convinced by the awful lesson here taught, 'that whatever wild or chimerical notions may prevail of the power of an armed multitude, the law is too strong for its assailants'.

Over a period of six days, some fifty-four rioters appeared before the judges. In all twenty-four were charged with capital offences of either burglary, robbery from the person or stealing in a dwelling house. On the fifth day of the trial, thirty of the defendants were gathered in the dock together, indicted for various felonies and misdemeanours. These prisoners were in effect bound over to keep the peace and ordered to give their own recognizance for £50 and to pay sureties of £20.

The remaining twenty-four prisoners were charged with the range of capital offences stated: Aaron Chevall, Richard Jessop, Joseph Easey, Robert Crabb, William Dann, Thomas South, George Crow, Robert Butcher, John Walker, and Mark Benton were all charged with robbery from a dwelling house. James Newell, Isaac Harley, John Dennis, John Jefferson, Richard Rutter, William Beamiss the younger, Hugh Evans, Aaron Layton, William Atkin, Sarah Hobbs, John Pricke, John Cooper, James Crammell and William Beamiss the elder were all charged with robbery from the person.

Details of individual actions and episodes during the riots were put forward during the trial, and were reported in local and national newspapers. At one point, a number of prisoners charged with stealing in the dwelling house of Mrs Waddelow were acquitted on a point of law, only to be retried for other offences. Much was made of the crime of stealing a set of silver spoons, which were produced as evidence in court, from the home of the Reverend Vachell. The irony of trying food rioters over the theft of a set of gravy spoons may well have been lost on the members of the jury at the time.

Of the twenty-four charged with, and found guilty of capital offences, five were picked out to face the gallows. Justice Abbott, in his address to the prisoners at the bar, declared that 'human justice requires that some of you should undergo the full sentence, in order that others may be deterred from following the example of your crimes'. At this point he called out the names of John Dennis, William Beamiss the elder, Isaac Harley, Thomas South and George Crow. The unfortunate five were assumedly singled out as ringleaders and perpetrators of the most seditious behaviour and violent crimes, although the accounts of the detail of their activities at the time appear to lend a degree of the arbitrary as well as a deal of misfortune in their selection. It is not clear for example, why George Crow, rather than John Easey, John Walker or Robert Butcher was singled out for execution for the crime of stealing in the dwelling house of Mrs Waddelow. Of the remaining prisoners, whose sentences were commuted, ten were sentenced to a year's imprisonment in Ely gaol and the rest were sentenced to transportation for between seven years and life. What was clear was the degree of sympathy from the public for the condemned men. As the time approached for the five to be brought to the gallows, no-one would lend the authorities a cart. The fact that a cart had to be brought-in from out of town stands as testament to a feeling that the executions were overly harsh.

After the sentences were passed, Justice Christian sought to reiterate the circumstances under which the riots took place. His words were recorded and reproduced in an article in the *Cambridge Chronicle and Journal* on the 28th June, and amount to an out and out denial of any hardship suffered by the defendants:

> the conduct of the rioters cannot be attributed to want or poverty; the prisoners were all robust men, in full health, strength and vigour, who were receiving great wages, and any change in the price of provisions could only lessen the superfluity which, I fear, they too frequently wasted in drunkenness.

Whilst it is fair to say that alcohol obviously played a big part in the progress of the riots, and much is made of reference to the labourers' demands for beer, the delightfully optimistic demands of Richard Rutter for beer at tuppence a pint being a good case in point, to dismiss these events as a mere manifestation of drunken euphoria would be to miss a key point of rural life. Up until the early nineteenth century, domestic brewing was a key part of life for the agricultural labourer, or more often than not, his wife. The poor quality of drinking water at the time was such that brewing beer at home was common practice, not least as a means of avoiding contamination. However, with the rapid increase in the number of enclosures contributing to a scarcity of fuel needed for brewing (as well as day-to-day cooking at home), together with the economic conditions already described, home brewing fell into decline shortly after the turn of the century, and villagers came to rely on public houses as suppliers of their beer. So in one sense, through their demands for bread and beer, the labourers were merely asking for commodities that they had enjoyed in greater volume during the more prosperous years before the Napoleonic Wars. What is interesting here, as would be seen in the cases of other riots over the years, is that the authorities were at pains to give the impression that rioters were engaging in their activities from a position of relative affluence, and not driven to riot through desperation and poverty. The addition of beer to the equation meant that it was easier to portray the rioters as 'drunkards' as well as avaricious criminals bent on destruction and oblivion.

That beer played a key role in the riots is still recognized in folk tradition today, as it was at the time. The 'Ely and Littleport Riot' lives on. Affectionately known as 'El Riot', Ely & Littleport Riot is a Fenland women's Morris Side ('side' being the correct term for a group of Morris dancers), based in the town of Littleport. With colourful costumes representing the black of the Fenland earth (black skirts) and the red of the blood that ran that day in 1816 (red scarves), El Riot meet regularly on a Friday and dance to a melody that celebrates and laments the actions of the rioters. To the tune of an old army recruitment song, 'over the hills and far away', perhaps known to many as the theme music from the TV Series *Sharpe's Rifles*, El Riot celebrate the events of years ago; 'eighteen sixteen was the year, the rioters marched for bread and beer. Exile or death for their deeds that day, over the fens to Botany Bay'. The modern telling highlights the plight of those convicted. I contacted El Riot through their website and was delighted to receive a reply from Maggie Kent, the 'fearless leader' of the Morris Side. Maggie put me in touch with Alan Battersby, one of the musicians, who has been involved with the group since its beginnings in the mid 1980s. Alan informed me that it was said locally that descendants of the 1816 rioters in Littleport used to be ashamed to admit the family connections, but it is now seen more as a source of pride. At the time of execution, some 5,000 people turned out to witness the event, which was considered a great spectacle. Three hundred local dignitaries on horseback and carrying white wands, followed the cart bearing the condemned to the drop. The five men were said to have demonstrated the utmost contrition and had signed an acknowledgement of the justice of their own sentences. A copy of their voluntary confession was made available to the public. Before execution, John Dennis addressed the assembled crowd and urged all to take heed of his and his companions' fate as a warning. His words urged the crowd against 'drunkenness, whoredom and Sabbath breaking', which he apparently maintained were the three main causes of his current predicament. Amid the spectacle of a carefully staged and managed public execution it is unlikely that Dennis, and his fellow condemned companions, would ever have had the opportunity to offer any other explanation leading to their actions in the riot. A detailed lecture on political economy, describing the miserable lot of the village labourer, was never really going to be the last words uttered from a man before the gallows. And so a whole series of hunger riots are easily dismissed and portrayed as the actions of a binge drinking, irreligious violent mob.

On a miserable spring day, I stood in the grounds of St Mary's Church in Ely in the pouring rain, gazing at a plaque mounted on the western wall of the small church. Carved in sandstone, are the names of the five who died on the gallows; Dennis, Beamiss, Harley, South and Crow. At the foot of the plaque reads, 'May their awful fate be a warning to others'. But I couldn't see the plaque, and what happened to those named there, as a warning. Like the members of El Riot, and the small display given over to the riots in Ely History Museum in the old school in the town centre, I saw the memorial plaque as a stark reminder of desperate times and desperate measures, one of suffering and sacrifice. I saw it more as a celebration of the bravery of a community which stood up for what it saw as a right to affordable food and a fair wage for their labours. The option for once legitimate protest in the market place had been severely curtailed towards the end of the previous century, as the authorities clamped down on food riots across the country. The disenfranchized and labouring poor of East Anglia took their protest to the streets and homes of those they saw as responsible for their plight. At the time, of course, the Ely and Littleport rioters, as well as those from further afield, were portrayed as work-shy, idle benefit scroungers looking for a free meal, in much the same way as are the unfortunate families queuing at food banks are today.

END NOTES

1. Burnett, J. *Plenty & Want: a social history of diet in England,* p.30.
2. Peacock, A.J. *Bread or Blood: the agrarian riots in East Anglia,* p.18.
3. Burnett, J. *Plenty & Want: a social history of diet in England,* p.32.
4. Plumb, J.H. *England in the Eighteenth Century,* p.82.
5. Peacock, A.J. *Bread or Blood: the agrarian riots in East Anglia,* p.43.
6. Ibid. p.49.
7. Ibid. p.97.
8. Johnson, C. *An account of the Ely & Littleport Riots,* p.14.
9. Peacock, A.J. *Bread or Blood: the agrarian riots in East Anglia,* p.106.
10. Johnson, C. *An account of the Ely & Littleport Riots,* p. 26.

CHAPTER THREE

CAPTAIN SWING AND THE RAGE AGAINST THE MACHINE (1830)

The 'Swing Riots' of 1830 are not generally considered as 'food riots' per se, so here I must lay out my case. The disturbances which spread over much of southern England in the latter part of 1830 are more often than not described as a labour and wages dispute, or in some cases as a reaction to growing poverty in rural areas. Given that those enduring such poverty – in addition to those whose circumstances were changed and often worsened by the advent of mechanized labour-saving devices, namely the threshing machine – found themselves struggling to place food on the table at home, I am fully prepared to offer the widespread 'Swing Riots' as one almighty food fight which was to have lasting consequences, and one which to a degree brought about Poor Law reform and arguably laid the foundations for the welfare state which was to come in the following century.

The 'Swing Riots' were the most widespread of all the food riots in the country in the nineteenth century. Whilst anger and much

70

violence was directed against the new threshing machines, which were rapidly being adopted as labour-saving devices among the country's farmers, it is remarkable that not one death occurred throughout their duration. A great deal of violence was involved, but no one was killed. The classic analysis of the 'Swing Riots' was put forward in 1969 by Hobsbawm and Rudé, and pins the origins of the movement to a farm in Lower Hardes in Kent, where in August 1830, the first threshing machine was destroyed with vigour by farm labourers from the surrounding villages. The date and exact location has since been contested in more recent studies, but in many ways such concern over detail is to a degree, immaterial. Hobsbawm and Rudé noted that protesters used an array of methods to convey their concerns over working conditions in the English countryside; arson, threatening letters, wage meetings, riotous assemblies gathered for the specific extraction of monies or provisions from farmers. Whilst machine breaking was the activity for which the riots are largely remembered, arson and the firing of corn, oats, barley and other cereals were by far the most widely used weapons in the rioters' armoury.

It is the reference to the machine breaking that has given rise to comparisons with the Luddite uprising in the industrial north of England a decade or so earlier in the century. Both disturbances were lead by mythical characters, Captain Swing is often said to be the grandson, or sometimes the rural cousin of General Ludd. The truth is there is little evidence to suggest that 'swing' was an actual person. The word swing served as a warning to farmers. Carl Griffin, historical geographer at the University of Sussex, suggests that swing was used as a violently suggestive metonym, which reflected both the swinging action of a threshing flail, and the much more sinister vision of a body swinging on a gibbet. The relationship between myth and legend is a dynamic which many have pondered, and in the case of the 'Swing Riots', I believe the two come in to play. The employment of a figurehead for any cause or uprising is clearly useful both in terms of a recruitment tool, as well as a means of concealing identities of those involved. The threatening letters to farmers, warning them to destroy or dismantle their threshing machines or face the consequences, were often signed by the mythological character, 'Captain Swing'. There is a fine line which separates myth from legend, torn, it seems, between historical legitimacy on the one hand, and fantasy on the other. To define that line with precision is an almost impossible task. For me, the deeds of some of those associated with the riots, in particular William Cobbett, appear to transgress the divide. Given that confusing myth with legend is tantamount to mixing the metaphor, I will tread carefully here, but I believe that there is some scope for myths and legends to become entwined when it comes to the 'Swing Riots' of 1830.

In his 2012 volume, *The Rural War*, Carl Griffin reiterates that 'Swing was born of the experience of pauperisation and impoverishment'.[1] This was a movement in which hunger and the fear of hunger played a significant role. In the towns and cities, the onset of the Industrial Revolution had done much to alter the role of the labourer. Mechanization in many cases was seen as displacing the jobs of the poor, and perhaps more so by the time that mechanization had found its way to the country farm. The precedent for destruction of machinery was set in the textile mills of the north of England, and was followed up in parts of the countryside during the 1820s.[2] Riots at this stage could almost certainly be seen as a reflection of growing unrest in the countryside, but as they did not spread, these disturbances were seen as isolated outbursts.

The 1820s did indeed witness a growth of political dissent and calls for a reconsideration of the Poor Laws. One such champion of the poor, or more specifically, champion of the country labourer was William Cobbett (1763-1835). As the son of a Hampshire farmer and one time publican, Cobbett had taken more than a passing interest in political and social reform. Exiled twice to America and tried for seditious libel in 1831, by the early 1820s he had become well established as a radical calling for both political and Poor Law reform. Through his weekly newspaper, *The Political Register*, which ran from 1802 right up until 1835, the year of his death, Cobbett had consistently mocked, chastized and goaded the political elite. *The Register* had gained Cobbett a loyal following among the labourers of southern England, and that popularity was cemented as throughout the 1820s he undertook a series of 'rural rides' through many of the counties of southern England. Often riding alone on horseback, or in the company of his son, Cobbett made copious notes on the 'state of the English countryside'. He recorded conversations with labourers and farmers alike. He noted wage levels and cereal prices at the time, the living conditions and diet of the poor became a focus of his attention. Accounts of many of these 'rides' and the adventures he undertook appeared in the pages of his newspaper, but the collection was bound and published in 1830 in what is perhaps his most famous book, *Rural Rides*. His timing seemed impeccable.

Through his first-hand experience of conditions in the countryside, Cobbett had predicted a rural uprising on an unprecedented scale, and by 1828, he was even confident enough to date that rebellion to the winter of 1830.[3] Cobbett's clairvoyance is legendary it seems, an attribute which could easily be given to a mythical character. Whilst the government at the time clearly thought otherwise, prosecuting Cobbett in 1831 for seditious libel following the publication in *The Political Register* of an article in support of the 'Swing Riots', modern historians hold that William Cobbett was not Captain Swing.

It is clear that Cobbett's writings had permeated the ranks of the country labourers, circulation figures for *The Register* were in the region of 40,000. Hobsbawm and Rudé note that, 'among the Hampshire radicals who played a leading part in the riots about Micheldever was William Winkworth, a shoe maker and former constable who was said to have read Cobbett's *Register* aloud to a 'small party of Hampshire bumpkins on Saturday nights.[4] It was events such as this, which led to Cobbett's trial in July of 1831. Choosing to offer his own defence, Cobbett was able to make much of a series of confessions obtained from a Kentish cooper by the name of Thomas Goodman. Goodman had been convicted of setting fire to a barn near Battle in Kent, and was sentenced to death. In his confession, Goodman had stated that he believed were it not for Cobbett and his 'lectures' to the country labourers, the series of arson attacks and machine breaking would not have occurred. Goodman then went on to offer more detailed confessions, all implicating Cobbett as having direct influence over the course of rioting. The fact that Goodman had received a royal pardon, and his sentence was commuted to transportation to Tasmania, shed an unfavourable light on the veracity of his confessions. In the offending article, titled 'Rural War', Cobbett had written that:

> Without entering at present into the motives of the working people, it is unquestionable that their acts have produced good, and great good too. They have always been told … that their acts of violence, and particularly the burnings can do them no good but to add to their wants, by destroying the food that they would have to eat. Alas! They know better; they know that one threshing machine take wages from ten men.[5]

Cobbett, like many of those more directly involved in the riots, could see good in their actions. In many cases, farmers raised wages and agreed to dismantle threshing machines as a direct result of the rioting. Cobbett was also able to produce a sworn affidavit at his trial, signed by the farmer whose barn Goodman had torched. It gave clear indication of the falsehood of Goodman's confession. The jury was unable to reach a majority verdict, and accordingly the case ended in acquittal and Cobbett walked free, doubtless with a swing in his step.

Having started in Kent in the August of 1830, the 'Swing Riots' quickly spread across much of southern England. The rioters were mainly young men or men of early middle age. Boys and old men were rare, and women in the vast minority. It is also true that as this was an uprising among labourers, the term 'labourer' itself was a 'catch all' term and covered a broad range of skills, among which were ploughmen, reapers, stable boys and milkmen. Shearers, porters, footmen and house servants also took part. Many of these 'professions' are detailed in legal proceedings against the rioters at the time and in their meticulous research, Hobsbawm and Rudé make reference to an unusual sounding profession, which caught my eye, a 'jobber in pigs and chickens' hailing from Wiltshire.[6]

Wages among this band of 'labourers' came in at around ten shillings per week, in some cases slightly more. In Wiltshire, however, the weekly wage was considerably lower at around seven shillings, and it was in Wiltshire that some of the most violent rioting took place, arson attacks in particular were prevalent in the county. The words, written in the 1980s, of Dorset based singer/songwriter Graham Moore, capture and help portray the desperation and anxiety of both the labouring man and the farmer during the uprising:

> The labouring man is on his knees, oh where can he get hired?
> Since new machines that do the work, the farmer has acquired.
> But how he sweats, when he reads the threats on paper morning brings,
> Destroy your gear or else I swear you'll pay, signed Captain Swing.

Wiltshire too was a frequent haunt of William Cobbett. Visiting the county on one of his rural rides in 1826, he was able to give accounts of the lot of the labourer just four years prior to the riots erupting. Travelling south along the Valley of Avon from Wattton Rivers (now Wootton Rivers) to Salisbury, Cobbett remarked 'I never before saw anything to please me like this valley of the Avon'. He described a land rich with crops:

> The turnips look pretty well all the way down the valley; but, I see very few except Swedish turnips. The early common turnips very nearly all failed, I believe. But, the stubbles are beautifully bright; and the rick-yards tell us that the crops are good, especially of wheat. The crops are wheat, barley, wool and lambs.[7]

Clearly visiting after an abundant harvest, his description and concerns for those labouring along the valley were less idyllic. Noting that the Valley of Avon produced such bounty, Cobbett pondered as to what would be the requirement for a family of five persons to live well; five pounds of bread per day, a pound of mutton and two pounds of bacon a day, a gallon and a half of beer. Sadly, the reality of the labouring man's diet was a very different story. He describes a real income of just nine shillings per week, a mere pittance and certainly not enough to keep the family work fit. 'Monstrous, barbarous, horrible as this appears', he says, 'we do not however see it in half its horrors'. 'Dogs and hogs and horses are treated with more civility; and as to food and lodging, how gladly would the labourers change with them!'[8]

In the years that followed, conditions grew considerably worse. Inclement weather and poor harvests, together with mechanization in the fields had reduced the lot of the labourer to little. By November of 1830, the momentum of the 'Swing Riots' had reached the Valley of Avon. The Wiltshire disturbances appear to have begun in Wilcot near Marlborough, with threatening 'Swing' letters delivered to farmers and land owners in the area. Fires were seen at Collingbourne, Easton and Ludgershall.

Historian Jill Chambers offers a wealth of local detail in her two volume study of *The Wiltshire Machine Breakers* that appears to highlight the solidarity of both the victims and the perpetrators of the riots:

> During the night all the wheat, barley, beans and oats belonging to Mr Fowler of Oare, near Pewsey, was destroyed by fire. Had it not been for the exertions of several respectable people of Pewsey, Mr Pontin's house and farm buildings would have shared a similar fate. One of them placed an engine between Mr Pontin's property and the fire. It has to be said that the labourers of Oare, instead of assisting to put out the fire appeared to take pleasure from the situation, and with the exception of very few, were laying about enjoying the scene. It was found necessary to place 12 Pewsey men to guard the water pipes after it was found that one of them had been cut. One of those fighting the fire has stated the belief that if it had not been for the Pewsey men there would not have been a house left standing in Oare and it is believed that the fire was the work of the labourers of the village.[9]

The image of labourers 'laying around' and enjoying the show must have enraged the unfortunate victims. A letter from a 'sincere well-wisher' to The Labourers of Wiltshire was widely distributed around

Devizes, Marlborough and Pewsey. It implored those to 'beware of men who are going about the county to make you do what you will soon be sorry for. The times are bad. But will burning corn make your situation more comfortable or give you bread?'[10] Such injunctions proved ineffective as more threatening 'Swing' letters were delivered and riots spread across the county, farmers were beginning to heed the warnings. Justices at Devizes had resolved that they would not accede to the demands of rioters until order had been restored, but this was not true of some local farmers who were quick to bargain with the mobs. Hobsbawm and Rudé cite a less than effective effort at such bargaining by an Amesbury farmer, James Judd. Judd offered beer and money to his assailants and asked for protection from other rioters in return. Sadly his negotiating skills were clearly lacking as after accepting the bribe, rioters returned later in the day and destroyed his threshing machine in a matter of five minutes.

Justices recommended that farmers increase the weekly wage to ten shillings. The rioters were gaining ground and it appeared that Cobbett was right, good would, and did, come of the disturbances. Mixed messages clearly abounded in the mayhem, and whilst concessions were gained, the fervour with which to apprehend offenders was also stepped up. The day after the labourers of Oare apparently enjoyed a warming celebration of their endeavours, a meeting was held in Marlborough town hall. Chambers again offers detail of the agenda, where a subscription was entered in to by those present to offer 'rewards for the apprehension and conviction of the persons who are destroying property by burning or otherwise'. The £400 raised at that meeting was clearly not enough to quell the activities of the local labourers. Just two days later on Monday 22 November, another meeting was convened in the Duke's Arms Inn in Marlborough. Here, a number of gentlemen were sworn-in as special constables, and a specific reward of £200 was offered for the conviction of those responsible for firing Mr Fowler's property at Oare.

Despite the mobilization of the Marlborough Troop of the Wiltshire Yeomanry, the numbers participating in the riots was increasing. Crowds gathered at Great Bedwyn, visiting a number of farms and extorting money and victuals from farmers. Many of the farmers had already dismantled their threshing machines, but this was often not enough to dissuade angry labourers from destroying machines beyond repair. In many cases, the complicity of the farmers was condemned by the upper classes, Lord Buckingham had complained that in certain areas, 'the farmers had not the spirit, and in some instances not the wish to put down the disturbances'.[11] Clearly, Lord Buckingham had not encountered an angry mob at first hand. By 23 November the numbers of protestors in Great Bedwyn had grown to some 800. Elsewhere a group of protestors convened on Fyfield, where they accosted a Miss Elizabeth Penrudduck. After carefully explaining that she was not a farmer, she implored the mob to leave. The crowd demanded two sovereigns and issued threats to Miss Penruddock, to the effect that 'we don't stand shilly shally here, my lady'.[12] Penrudduck paid up and the crowd moved on. What is remarkable is the sheer numbers of rioters who took part in the protests, and the authorities' concerns are perhaps reflected in a number of proclamations posted stipulating rewards offered for the capture of those participating. Sums of up to £50 were offered for the apprehension and conviction of rioters, while a whopping £500 was offered in respect of arsonists. A similar situation presented itself across many of the counties in southern England. The rapid nature of the spread of the riots, together with the wilful enthusiasm of the participants, gave the authorities deep cause for concern. Aside from arson and the destruction of machinery, rioters had taken to visiting the homes of unpopular dignitaries. Demands for money and beer were made as rioters delivered their 'rough music' to those in the community seen to be in a position to afford or deserve it. As the winter pressed on, magistrates and law enforcement agencies were given to gaoling anyone who was deemed to be a trouble maker. Gaols across the south of England were full to bursting and by December, the 'Swing Riots' had all but died out.

Historians Hammond and Hammond record that while the disturbances were over, the upper classes were still in a state of panic. As late as Christmas Eve, the Privy Council issued orders to the archbishop to prepare a form of prayer to God Almighty. It seemed that divine providence, as well as the long arm of the law was required to calm things down, and the passage prepared by the archbishop reads thus:

> Restore, O Lord to Thy people the quiet enjoyment of the many and great blessings which we have received from Thy bounty: defeat and frustrate the malice of wicked and turbulent men, and turn their hearts: have pity O Lord, on the simple and ignorant, who have been lead astray, and recall them to their sense of duty ...

The 'simple and the ignorant' were soon to learn of what would become of them. Reprisals across the affected counties were swift, and in Wiltshire, at the start of the special Assizes convened in Salisbury on 27 December, some 300 names ware put before the magistrates. The trial took place in January 1831, and many of the prisoners found themselves in a difficult situation as the only witnesses to their individual behaviour, were also part of the mob. Any witness brave enough to testify would therefore be committed too, as they would be seen by the judge as having taken part in the riot. Such was the case concerning the trial of a certain James Lush, whose only witness chose to remain silent for fear of being indicted himself. In effect, it was a matter of many of those accused having to face the law without legal representation. During the trial, which lasted eight days, one hundred and four men were sentenced to transportation. Forty seven were sentenced to death, although forty four of those had their sentences commuted to transportation. Of the three remaining, Peter Withers and James Lush were reprieved and were transported for life. In addressing the Grand Jury, Mr Justice Park spoke of the authorities having witnessed a spirit of insubordination and tumult, spreading from similar outbreaks in many parts of the kingdom.

He described scenes of violence and outrage against property and assemblages of persons in a state nearly amounting to rebellion. And herein lies a clue suggesting the fear among the authorities that all out rebellion or revolution was seen as a likely outcome of the riots. Hammond and Hammond describe the scenes of sorrow and terror in the court room at the close of the trial; one man begged to be allowed to take his eight-month-old child into exile with him as the mother had died and there was no family to look after him. The judge refused his pleas. Mothers and wives rushed, shrieking to the dock to shake hands as a final farewell to their loved ones destined for transportation. It was not just those convicted that felt the full weight of the law, but villages and communities across the county were devastated as the wage earners were banished from the country. But it's clear that Captain Swing's cards were marked from the beginning. Following the 'Swing Riots', over 2,000 people appeared before the special assizes, and some 500 prisoners were transported from the counties of southern England. After having been assembled on the prison hulks moored in the Thames estuary and in ports on the South Coast, the majority of the Swing rioters set sail for New South Wales and Van Dieman's Land (Tasmania) in 1831.

Historian Peter Higginbotham captures the essence of the riots and the fate of those involved in his 'Ballad of Captain Swing', written in 2003.

> In eighteen hundred and twenty nine
> The summer was wet and the sun would not shine,
> The terrible harvest was surely a sign –
> An omen for Captain Swing.
>
> *Chorus*
> Oh Captain Swing, he'll come in the night,
> To set all your buildings and crops alight,
> And smash your machines with all his might,
> That dastardly Captain Swing!
>
> The following year was just as bad
> No corn to be reaped and no work to be had.
> Poor labouring men were driven quite mad
> And rallied to Captain Swing.
> They cried to the farmers to take heed,
> These threshing machines are the last thing we need,

If you must persist in doing this deed.
You'll soon hear from Captain Swing

And all through the heart of this fair land,
The call went abroad for justice to stand.
Men rose up and marched to make their demand
In the name of Captain Swing.

From Norfolk to Berkshire went the cry,
For food in our bellies we'll gladly die.
Machines were smashed up and fires lit the sky,
As promised by Captain Swing.

As poor men assembled and attacked,
The justices read out the Riot Act.
T'was soon clear the odds were heavily stacked
Contrary to Captain Swing.

The leaders were charged and guilty found,
Some were deported and some scaffold bound,
But true working men forever should sound
The praises of Captain Swing.

The suggestion that 'true working men should sound the praises of Captain Swing' is born out in what happened in the years that followed.

Most surprisingly, by 1834, the majority of those convicted were offered a royal pardon. The pardons issued were perhaps riding on the back of the success of those campaigning on behalf of the 'Tolpuddle Martyrs', a group of farm workers in West Dorset who had banded together to form a workers' union. Unions were at the time illegal and six of the leaders were sentenced to transportation for seven years following their arrest. The huge public outcry at the time lead to a reprieve and the martyrs returned, in triumph to Dorset. In the case of the Swing rioters transported a couple of years earlier many opted, or more likely had not the means to return, to stay in what was to become Australia. A number of the Swing rioters were able to return to England and to take up life where they had left off. The country, to which the few returned, was a changing one, and the 'Swing Riots' of 1830 had played a significant role in that change. Eric Hobsbawm highlighted this year as one which marks a turning-point in the wave of major political and social change. It was a wave, and swept across a great many of European countries during this period. It seems difficult to imagine that the efforts of the Swing rioters, and those who campaigned for clemency on the rioters' behalf, were not instrumental in bringing about the Representation of the People Act of 1832. Known as the Reform Act, this series of reform bills ushered in a series of significant changes to the constitution of the United Kingdom. The Act created 130 new seats in parliament, and extended the franchise to land owners and leaseholders with land way below the value of that held by the 'landed gentry' for the first time. The Act fell well short of empowering the likes of those who had been transported, but it marked a somewhat reluctant recognition, on behalf of the establishment, of a pressing need for political and social reform.

As well as offering limited concessions through a small extension of the franchise, the Reform Act of 1832 saw the demise of the 'rotten boroughs' – a system whereby members of parliament were able to take up a seat in the House of Commons with little or no representation from the electorate. This was a system which William Cobbett and other radicals and reformists had long since been campaigning against. Though far short of the political system we know today, the Reform Act marked a change under which conditions of the poor and the working classes would slowly begin to improve. Charles Grey became prime minister in 1830. Earl Grey was a keen supporter of reform, and was noted as one of the instigators of the Reform Act of 1832. By 1834, pardons had been granted to the Swing rioters themselves, largely as a result of the efforts of family members and other campaigners gathering petitions. The pardons give the impression of a recognition of the harsh conditions under which many of those who took part in the riots were living and can perhaps be seen as an extension of the 'spirit of reform' which abounded at the time. Further recognition around this period appears through an increase in the allocation of allotments to the landless poor, for the purposes of growing food for their own subsistence. The allotment movement in England originated in 1793,[13] arguably as a counterweight to the rapid expansion of enclosure, but it owes a great deal to the efforts of the 'Swing Riots' of 1830. By allocating land to labourers on which to grow their own food, reformists and campaigners argued that the poor would be less tied to the wages and less susceptible to fluctuations in food prices, and this might tackle, in part at least, one of the problems that caused people to riot in the first place. Calls for the allocation of land for the poor on which to cultivate their own food had emerged in previous centuries, in particular as a response to the expansion of enclosure. Although a broad brush approach to the allocation of allotments was never taken up by the government, those allocations which were made were often at the behest of local members of the clergy, or benevolent land owners such as Lords Winchilsea and Carrington. One of the arguments at the time, against the idea of allotments for the poor, and one which was held by a number of farmers, was that they would limit the mobility of labour. A person tending their allotment might not be available to till the farmer's fields or to work in the new mills and factories springing up across the country. Farmers and shopkeepers were also reluctant to see a spread of allotments as the poor would conceivably be less inclined to rely on both for the provision of food for the table. Those who had made allotment provision were keen to broadcast the results of their schemes, most notably a reduction in the cost to the local parish in terms of poor relief. So by 1830, the allocation of allotments was arguably seen as an effective method of poor relief. Jeremy Burchardt, in his study of the Allotment Movement, has noted what he calls a 'geographical fit' with the renewal of interest in allotments and the counties affected by the 'Swing Riots'. He also notes that 1830-1831 was the beginning of a period of 'sustained growth' of the allotment movement. The links are there to see. The first Select Committee on allotments was not convened until more than a decade later in 1843, but even then it harked back to the events of 1830 in one of its early reports stated that:

> it was not until 1830, when discontent had been so painfully exhibited amongst the peasantry of the southern counties, that this method [the allocation of allotments] of alleviating their situation was much resorted to.

In other words, very little was done until labourers desperate with hunger had set the countryside alight.[14] What is interesting about some of the allotment allocations made in the early part of the nineteenth century, is the apparent connection, or association at least, with the Swing rioters of 1830.

In Marlborough, Wiltshire for example, as well as in Church Cowley, near Oxford, the areas of land given over to allotments was given the name 'Van Dieman's Land', or 'Van Dieman's Allotments'. Whether this was a deliberate monument to the toils of the Swing rioters, or the land was named at a later date is difficult to ascertain, but in some ways it sits as a gentle reminder of what the rioters achieved. Clearly many paid dearly and never saw their homelands again, but the immediate effect of the rioters' actions across much of southern England in 1831 – local wage increases, farmers willingly destroying or ceasing to use their own threshing machines was there for all to see. The majority of those transported did not get to see the more lasting legacy of the 'Swing Riots'. Only the few that made their way back to England would have seen first hand what they and their colleagues had achieved. The Representation of the People Act of 1832 and the conciliatory atmosphere leading to the royal pardon for rioters in 1834, together with the Poor Law reforms of 1834 were indicative of the fact that the poor were beginning to be seen as a collective body, and a body which might rise and affect the livelihood of the upper classes. These food rioters had clashed with the establishment, and were banished overseas for their actions.

That the most widespread food riots of the nineteenth century began in the English countryside and ended with the protagonists being transported far overseas, seems poignant. The destruction and upheaval of the next food fight in this compendium occurred at the end of the same century, and was one which took place in the seas and the coastline of Cornwall.

END NOTES

1. Griffin, C. *The Rural War, Captain Swing and the politics of protest*, p.7.
2. Ibid. p.53.
3. Dyck, I. *William Cobbett and rural popular culture*, p. 152.
4. Hobsbawm, E.J. & Rudé, G. *Captain Swing*, p.246.
5. Cited in Ingrams, R. *The Life and Adventures of William Cobbett*, p.234/235.
6. Hobsbawm, E.J. & Rudé, G. *Captain Swing*, p.243.
7. Cobbett, W. *Rural Rides*, p.280.
8. Ibid. p.296.
9. Chambers, J. *Wiltshire Machine Breakers*, 1993.
10. Hobsbawm & Rudé, *Captain Swing*, p. 124.
11. Cited in Hammond & Hammond, *The Village Labourer*, p.265.
12. Chambers, J. *Wiltshire Machine Breakers*, 1993.
13. Burchardt, J. The Allotment Movement in England 1793-1873.
14. Hammond & Hammond, *The Village Labourer*, p.161.

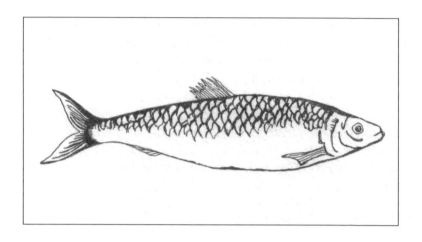

CHAPTER FOUR

THE ORIGINAL FISH FIGHT

The Newlyn Fish Riots of 1896

Like many coastal settlements, the fishing village of Newlyn in Cornwall owes its existence to the violent forces of plate tectonics and the movement of the earth's crust. Taking its name in part from the old Cornish word *lyn* meaning 'pool', the village lies at the eastern edge of the natural deep waters of Gwavas Lake at the western end of what is today known as the English Channel. With an ancient, colourful, and at times violent history as a fishing village, Newlyn stands as an important benchmark for the rest of the country, not least because height above sea level in the United Kingdom is measured against the Ordnance Datum, found on the tide gauge bolt at Newlyn Pier.

Historical reference to the Cornish fishing industry first appears in the Domesday Book of 1086, with reference to the salt works of the region, salting being a method of preserving fish. In his great biography of *Cornwall and its People* (Dent & Sons Ltd: 1945), A.K. Hamilton Jenkin writes of licence being granted by King John in the early thirteenth century, to the French merchants of Bayonne to fish in Cornish waters. The French brought with them salt for preserving their catch, as well as improved material for building nets, paving the way for the rapid growth of the industry. More detailed accounts of the West Country fishermen appear in Richard Carew's *Survey of Cornwall* (1602) as he describes a coast plentifully stored with 'Brets, Turbets, Mackrell, Pilcherd, Herring, Tunny' and many other fish. Carew goes to great length in describing, not only the seemingly abundant array of species of fish and shellfish being harvested at the time, but also the methods by which fish were caught. He describes 'drouers' (drovers, or drivers) hanging 'certaine square nets athwart the tyde' to catch Pilchard.

Even in Elizabethan times it seems that conflict between fishermen over methods used to haul a catch were rife. Carew tells of how 'Sayners' (fishermen using seine nets) 'complayne with open mouth, that these drouers worke much preiudice to the Commonwealth of fishermen'. The seiners were apparently disgruntled with the 'drouers', whose methods not only caused schools of fish to scatter and disperse, but the quality of the catch once landed was poor due to the 'bruising' of fish caught in the drove nets.

Seine fishing at the time was, as Carew describes, 'the fashion'. A 'sayne' consisted of up to four boats at sea and a crew of watchers, or 'huers' situated on high cliffs with a view over the water and approaching shoals of fish. On the huer's instruction, a cry or signal from the cliff top, the fishermen would lower their nets as the shoal approached, and use their oars to beat the surface of the water, driving the fish into the nets. The 'fashion' was an efficient and enduring one, as seine fishing lasted right up until the twentieth century.

Aside from the perils of an arduous life at sea, Cornish fishermen were also subject to often violent occupational hazards such as kidnapping and piracy. While England was at war with France and Spain, West Country fishermen were seen, by foreign sailors as a potential source of information on the whereabouts and movements of the British naval fleet, they often fell victim to kidnapping by the enemy. Piratical practice was also not uncommon, with reports of pirates from as far afield as Algeria operating off the coast of England, seizing fishing boats and harassing merchant shipping. It wasn't until the late seventeenth century and the rise of the British navy that the waters off British shores were deemed less hazardous and prone to attack from foreign vessels.

It is of little surprise then that the hard working West Country fishermen were keen to secure the odd day off in the working week. In 1622, as Jenkin notes, record is found in the borough accounts to the effect that 'no owner of boats or nets shall dry or set their nets or owners of seines row to stem the Sunday night or any time before day of that night'.[1] The practice, among fishermen at least, of observing the Sabbath is clearly laid out. It was a custom that would last well into the nineteenth century, though not without challenge along the way.

As fishing practices and methods changed over time, disputes among practitioners of the trade naturally arose on the odd occasion. The differences and disputes between the 'seiners' and the 'drovers' or drifters, for example, often within the same port or fishing ground, gave way to challenges from further afield. Challenges would come not only to the Sabbatarian practice of choosing not to land fish on a Sunday, but also, and perhaps of more significance, to the mechanics of local markets and the English fishing trade as a whole. Significantly, those presenting the challenge came not from abroad, but from further along the coast.

By the nineteenth century the port of Newlyn had grown to become the largest fishing port in England, such that in 1802, some West Country share fishermen were said to have been earning up to eighteen shillings a week.[2] The prominence of Newlyn as a fishing port was largely due to the natural deep waters of Gwavas Lake, which provided a haven for boats while waiting to land their catches. Another factor was the neglect by other English fishing ports of the market for herring. At the time more herring was landed in the West Country than in the ports of the East Coast, although this was to change in later years.

Pilchards, herring and mackerel were the mainstay of Newlyn's fishing industry. Well into the nineteenth century there were in the region of 200 seines, operating off the Cornish coast. With the home market being limited, the pilchards landed at Newlyn were often sold for consumption abroad, the majority of the catch heading for the markets of Italy. In addition to the men at sea, the fishing industry supported a vast cohort of land-based workers, consisting mostly of women and children who were involved in salting, packing and pressing the fish. Rope makers, net makers, shipwrights, sail makers, blacksmiths and merchants all benefitted from the prosperous trade in fish. With the coming of the railway in 1859, the trade in fish and fish oil grew rapidly. Capacity to deliver fish more quickly over greater distances opened up new markets. In particular, demand for Cornish spring mackerel grew to such an extent that new, faster boats, luggers, were being built to service this new market. The new luggers brought with them new fishing methods, which would have far-reaching consequences that would ultimately see the village of Newlyn capturing headlines across the country.

By the late nineteenth century, the practice of observing the Sabbath had been established and adhered to by Newlyn men and women for well over 200 years. In May 1896, this antiquated practice appeared to be the flashpoint for a riot which lasted for three days. Since the building of the Cornish Railway, which brought access to a broader market, the Newlyn fishermen had long endured increasing competition at sea from fishing boats sailing from Lowestoft and Yarmouth as well as other ports. The East country fishermen, keen to exploit the benefits of the new steam transport, were landing their catch in the port of Newlyn. The blow to Newlyn men came not only from the new trawling fishing methods employed by the East coasters, often said to have caused great disruption and damage to the nets of the local drifters, but was compounded by the fact that the visitors were more than happy to land their catch on a Sunday.

Determined to see that the East coasters, or 'Yorkers' as they were known, should not land their fish on the Sabbath, it appears that a number of local men rowed out to meet one of the Lowestoft boats moored in the bay. After boarding the visiting trawler, the Newlyn men proceeded to throw the entire catch of mackerel (some total of 100,000 fish according to local newspaper reports) overboard. Things appear to have escalated from this point forward and caught the attention of the local constabulary, as well as regional and national newspapers. Reports from a number of newspapers at the time indicate that the ensuing riot lasted for three days and on the second day (Monday) as some of the East coasters made for Penzance to land their catch there, having been warned of the mayhem in Newlyn harbour, an advance by the Newlyn men on the port was repelled by both local police and the Penzance fishwives. Vastly outnumbered, the local police appealed to magistrates to telegraph for reinforcements from both the army and the navy. Three naval gunboats, HMS Ferret, HMS Curlew and HMS Traveller were dispatched to the area, together with a company of 350 soldiers from the 2nd Berkshire Regiment under the command of a Major Hassard.

According to a report in *The Cornishman* of the 21 May 1896, photographers who took snapshots of the events were compelled to deliver up their negatives, lest they be used for purposes of identification, similarly a local reporter was ushered off the scene by the gathering mob. Contemporary news reports are therefore somewhat confusing and appear to differ greatly in the reporting of chronological detail.

Many of the newspaper accounts of events were based on a number of telegraphs sent by East Coast agents based in Penzance, to their employers in Lowestoft. A Mr Capps, agent for a Lowestoft company, which owned 45 boats, claimed that the Lowestoft boat, 'Felix', was boarded by 3 or 400 Newlyn men, and that mackerel from a total of 14 boats was thrown into the sea. He also claimed that within 3 hours, the crowd had grown to 1000 strong. Given that the population of Newlyn at the time was around 1400, it appears that nearly the whole village was involved. The Newlyn men blockaded the harbour, raising a chain across the mouth to prevent those boats already inside from leaving. A later telegram, presumably from the same origins was sent to Lowestoft Member of Parliament H.S. Foster:

Cornishmen still throwing Lowestoft fish overboard. Newlyn harbour blocked, our crews held prisoner by Cornishmen ... sure life and property will be lost if not stopped at once.

A certain slapstick element in the affray appeared as the Newlyn fishermen attempted to board more visiting boats as they approached the harbour, and were pelted with fresh fish as they came alongside the 'Yorker' boats. Projectiles of a more harmful nature were used by the skippers of other Lowestoft boats, in the form of ballast stones, which must have caused some injury to their victims.

As well as at sea, disturbances were taking place on land. Rioters broke up empty fish boxes on the quayside, which were presumed to be there to pack the 'Yorker' catch. Police Inspector Matthews was injured by a flying fish box, while another constable appeared to have suffered injuries having been thrown from a cart. The Harbourmaster of Newlyn, a Mr. William Strick, was attacked by an angry mob after having set to sea to warn off more approaching Lowestoft trawlers. The rioters appeared largely to be made up of the younger population, with scuffles breaking out on a field on the edge of the village opposite the convalescent home (a handy location for the unfortunate victims). Colourful detail of the raid on Penzance describes a 200-strong mob of Newlyn and St Ives men intent on trashing the catch landed in the harbour there. Thirty special policemen were sworn-in on the spot as the Sabbath observers raised chants of 'we're here to take away your husbands'. The mob was met by the newly recruited officers of the law as well as posse of volunteers from Penzance made up of women and children. Their response to the taunts of the approaching mob was 'you can't do it for the life of you'. One unfortunate woman was said to have suffered an 'unmanly' smack in the face. The march on Penzance was repelled by heavy police baton, and the rioters returned to Newlyn.

The arrival of 350 soldiers and a number of naval gunboats by the second day of rioting, helped to quell the melee, although it appears that the members of the local Paul Parish Brass Band had other ideas. The sound of the band playing 'Jon the Bone', a traditional Helston

'Furry' dance tune, to which young men and old women danced in the dust of the quayside, must have engendered an almost carnival atmosphere to the goings-on. 'Jon the Bone was walking home, when he met with Sally Dover. He kissed her once then he kissed her twice, and he kissed her three times over'.

Appeals for calm were given by the older men of the village, as soldiers from the Berkshire Regiment occupied the quayside and blocked the entrance to the harbour from land. The chain blocking the harbour mouth was lowered and the damaged 'Yorker' boats were allowed to leave.

More fights occurred the following day, as apparently an unfortunate Lowestoft man found himself surrounded by a 'howling mob of Newlyn youths'. His assailants knocked him down and beat him with their sticks. That the 'Newlyn Riots' were seen by the local youth as a legitimate playground appears qualified in further newspaper reports of 'young braves' from Penzance gathering to join the affray.

Evidence of the enthusiastic participation by the local youth, as well as the existing rivalry between Penzance and Newlyn, in the riots is indicated in a piece which appeared about a month after the event. A local Primitive Methodist minister, Rev W. Vaughn wrote in *The Cornishman* in June of 1896, describing the attack on Penzance:

Excitement naturally was created and large crowds of people gathered together, which to their credit can be described (by personal observation) as orderly with no disposition to riot or ill-treat anyone. Unfortunately ill feeling was introduced into the affair, largely by the apparent hostile attitude which many of the leading men of Penzance took towards Newlyn; this gave rise to friction between the two places causing some little conflict between the younger people.

The reverend Vaughn's account goes on to reiterate, that while the men of Newlyn were later regretful of their actions, they felt that they had just cause in fighting for their right of Sunday rest.

By the Wednesday, some three days after the first fish were thrown, things were quiet enough such that half of the troops were withdrawn and Inspector Matthews and his twenty weary constables were able to leave the scene for a well earned rest, having been continuously on duty since Monday morning.[3]

The riots had attracted wide coverage by newspapers across the country, especially in the fishing ports of the East Coast. Newspapers from as far away as Aberdeen carried news of the events in Newlyn, and interest grew as to the outcome and reprisals that might follow from the authorities. From the outset, Members of Parliament were aware of the fracas. H.S Foster, MP for Lowestoft first brought the matter to the attention of the House on the 18th May. On the 21st May John Colomb, MP for Yarmouth asked the Home Secretary whether he would cause a special inquiry to be made into the conduct of the local authority at Newlyn. More specifically whether they had used their powers to protect the East coast fishermen and whether effective measures would be taken to ensure the conviction and punishment of the ringleaders.[4]

Reprisals followed fairly swiftly, as investigations into the riots took place before county magistrates at Penzance. The process of bringing those involved to justice within such a small community, and the consequences of any punishments metered out were clearly considered by the courts. Summonses were served on a number of Newlyn men, some of whom were at sea at the time of issue.

Of those summoned, nine men were tried in the Assizes at Bodmin in June of 1896; Thomas Hoskin, Nicholas Hoskin, John Giles Richards, William Tonkin, George Glasson, William Mann, William Triggs, Alfred Green and Thomas Harvey were all charged with rioting on the 18th, 19th and 20th of May 1896.

Together with a large number of evil disposed persons unknown, unlawfully, riotously and routously did assemble and gather together to disturb the public peace, and then unlawfully, riotously, routously and tumultuously, did make a great noise, riot, tumult and disturbance to the great terror and disturbance of Her Majesty's subjects there being and residing, passing and re-passing Newlyn Harbour in or near the parish of Paul.[5]

Green, Harvey, Hoskin and Triggs were further indicted with assaulting a Mr. George Reynolds, Master of the Lowestoft boat 'Warrior' on May 19, and assaulting police Inspector Matthews and Constable Spear on the same day. All pleaded not guilty. Prosecuting on behalf of the Treasury, were a Mr J. H. Foote and Fraser McLeod, acting for the defence were a Mr H. E. Duke and F. Bodily.

The town of Bodmin was said to be awash with fishermen and their friends who had arranged to stay throughout the duration of the trial. The public gallery was packed. At the first hearing on the Saturday, Thomas Harvey was acquitted. As the court adjourned, the remaining prisoners, with the exception of William Triggs, were granted bail to appear the following Monday. On resumption of proceedings, the accused were indicted on a number of counts including, causing a riot, causing a rout, and unlawful assembly. The men plead guilty to unlawful assembly, but not guilty to the other counts. Triggs and Mann were further charged with riotous assault upon Inspector Matthews and PC Spear. The unfortunate Mr. Triggs, who had seemed to have been singled-out as a ringleader, is more than likely to have been an overenthusiastic participant in affairs, together with Mr Tonkin were further charged with rioting on Wednesday 20 May as well. Again a plea of not guilty to charges, other than unlawful assembly was entered.

Throughout proceedings it became clear that through the testimony of witnesses, it was not possible to 'pin down' the exact movement and whereabouts of the accused during the alleged assaults on the police officers and the unfortunate Lowestoft fisherman, Mr. Reynolds. The judge, Mr Justice Lawrence, was however satisfied that the majority of the accused at least, were present during the whole affair.

Given the severity of the charges, what followed in the Judge's summing up and sentencing was truly remarkable. Careful consideration to the ramifications of any sentence had clearly been given by both prosecuting and defending lawyers, with reiteration from the side of the defence, that the men did not set out to do harm, but were merely acting to prevent the landing of fish on the Sabbath day in keeping with their custom.

The men were Bound Over to keep the peace and allowed to walk free from the court. This marks a significant deviation from the course of sentencing followed by judges trying food rioters in earlier years. Whether this leniency came about as a result of the machinations of the political geography of the region, or it perhaps marked a shift in tolerance towards this sort of behaviour is unclear. What is clear is that the defence put on a good show. The scenes in the gallery must have been jubilant to say the least. On reaching Penzance railway station in the evening, the men were met by a large crowd, among whom were a number of disgruntled Penzance men offering hisses and insult. Reaching Newlyn some time after they were greeted by scenes of jubilation, 'a bevy of young Miriams in holiday attire went forth to meet the heroes.'[6] Streets were lined with bunting. Flags, quilts, tablecloths and in some cases women's underwear (presumably freshly laundered) were hung from windows throughout the village. The ever-present Paul Parish band played sweet music into the evening, and the harbour was decorated with candles, fairy lights and Chinese lanterns. It must have been a hell of a party.

Whilst it may have had the appearance of a 'flash in the pan', the 'Newlyn Riots' must be seen in the context of a long struggle between local fishermen and the gradual encroachment of competition from fishing fleets from further afield. They differ somewhat from the nature of previous food riots, in that the participants were not starving or hungry at the time. Cloaked in what was seen by some as a 'religious' dispute over the landing of fish on the Sabbath, the disruption of May 1896 clearly carried a number of economic, as well as ecumenical concerns.

At the time, a call for compensation came from the Lowestoft boat owners, with sums amounting to thousands of pounds. The County Council applied to the Crown for reimbursement of the expenses incurred through hosting the 350 soldiers of the Berkshire Regiment. The application was refused. The matter of compensation for the East

Coasters, though it never came about, as well as the perceived leniency of the sentences, was debated in the House of Commons for some time after the event. A letter in *The Cornishman* newspaper, signed by 'a sufferer' attempted to put a monetary value on the cost of the disturbances:

> Sir – as the curtain has dropped on the first chapter of this unfortunate drama, it may not be amiss to pause and reckon the cost and its probable results. The annexed figures are given as an approximate and not with any intention of exaggeration.

The letter goes on to present the cost of fish thrown overboard at £900, the loss of a week's fishing with 250 boats laying idle £2,500, fleets still ashore (during the trial) £400 and the expenses of the trial itself at £700. 'The sufferer' cites a total of £4,500 having been lost and goes on to predict a loss of a further £10,000 as the withdrawal of 200 East Coast boats would effectively cripple the port of Newlyn.

In the period between the quelling of the riot and the sentencing of participants, agents from both the Cornish fishing industry and the East Coast companies had met in London in an attempt to settle the issue of landing fish on a Sunday. The conference amounted to little, and at the time, the secretary of the Lowestoft Boat Owners Association, A.B. Capps, remarked that the affair appeared as 'Sabbatarianism mixed with commercialism' and that the flavour of the latter was dominant, suggesting that there was less concern with landing fish on a Sunday, more with selling them on a Monday.

The coming of the railway to Cornwall had clearly brought about a great change on the market in fish as a whole. The advent of new trawl fishing methods brought large numbers of product to market, as well as concerns (which might seem relevant today) for the viability of fish populations. Sometimes, up to 300 tons of mackerel per day were loaded onto the train at Penzance. In this light, attribution of the origin of the 'Newlyn Riots', solely to that of a 'religious' dispute seems somewhat short sighted. Whilst the call for visiting fishermen to observe the Sabbath must have been certainly affected and to an extent driven by the desire to uphold an age old custom or religious practice (another dimension of E.P. Thompson's 'moral economy' if you like), it appears more prudent to see it as a means of challenging what must have been seen by many local fishermen, as a loss of access to new markets, and in particular the capacity to have fish for sale in Billingsgate market on a Monday morning.

Cornishman and playwright Nick Darke picked up on the ecclesiastical versus economic dispute in the disturbances, in his 1999 play based on the events of the 'Newlyn Fish Riots'. The impact of the riot, particularly among the families of those involved, was obviously considered at the time, and whilst events associated with the ruckus may have brought a degree of 'shame' on the community of Newlyn, reported and written about at length in contemporary newspaper reports, it was also clear to the families of fishermen who were affected by events that a way of life was hanging in the balance. Nick Darke's play *The Riot* is focussed around the efforts of local magistrate, MP, merchant banker and mine owner, Thomas Bolitho. In the play, Bolitho is caught between his loyalty and respect for the local fisherman, and the desire to ensure that Newlyn remains a viable fishing port. Bolitho is keen to placate the angry East Coast fishing agent Mr Capps, particularly when Capps threatens to take his business to another port, 'my god is mackerel, market day is mass and I'm the ruddy Pope and when the Pope is barred from Rome 'e buggers off to Plymouth.'[7] Whilst clearly it is Darke's own take on the riots that is being played out on the stage, and actual historic events are subject to artistic licence in this case, key community members such as Thomas Bolitho and the harbour master William Oats Strick, must have been torn between local loyalties and the responsibilities of their professional positions. Mr Capps' urgent telegraph messages to London and his demands for a military presence to quell the riot ('sure life and property will be lost if not stopped at once') certainly indicate the monetary value of the East Coast fishing operations, as does the amount of time given over in parliament to debating the issue. As far as the locals were concerned, it was a way of life that they were fighting for, both in the sense of wishing to preserve the sanctity of the Sabbath, as well as preserving the longevity of their fishing port.

The harbourmaster, William Strick was another who found himself in an unenviable position as the chaos came to a head. I met with a descendant of Strick's over a beer and a large bowl of fried whitebait, which seemed apt considering the nature of our conversation. David Matthews is the great great nephew of William Oats Strick. I'd been kindly put in touch with David by Pam Lomax of the Newlyn Archive, as I'd been making tentative enquiries via her website. David agreed to meet me at a pub in North Yorkshire which, though a world removed from Cornwall, served as a mutually convenient rendezvous. We began our conversation by pouring over David's meticulous research into his family history. There in the family tree was the name of the gentleman I'd been looking for. William Oats Strick was born in 1862. The 'Oats' part of his name, I was fascinated to learn, was his mother's maiden name. As well as holding the position of harbourmaster in Newlyn at the age of just 34, William Oats (as David referred to him) together with his brothers, owned up to 12 fishing boats over a period of some years. One of these may have been The Temperance Star, PZ259, a 48 foot, first class lugger, which was registered to William's older brother Charles Strick.[8] It is highly unlikely, David insisted, that the brothers owned twelve boats at any one time, as harbourmaster, William Strick earned a salary of £100 per year.[9] His shares in the fishing boats would have supplemented the income from his substantive post. From this information, it does not take an enormous stretch of the imagination to assume that William would indeed have had great empathy for the fishermen of his village. His role as harbourmaster, charged among other things, with the orderly upkeep of the tiny fishing harbour, placed him in a way, between a rock and a hard place. That he appeared to be a man of principle and stuck to his duties is born out by the fact that the villagers apparently attacked him and threatened him with arson after he had put to sea to warn the remaining Yorker fleet of the disruption in Newlyn harbour.

The 'Newlyn Fish Riots' differ significantly from those that took place elsewhere in the country and at an earlier date, but similarities can be drawn. The men and women here, whilst perhaps poor, were not necessarily hungry. This was not merely a 'rebellion of the belly', as E.P. Thompson might have called it. The folk of Newlyn were not driven to action by an immediate lack of food. They were, however, concerned for their way of life. They could see the threat to their livelihood coming as a result of industrialization, and chose to take action in their defence. In this respect, the Newlyn rioters shared a commonality with those who at the beginning of the century had taken to machine breaking. However, unlike the Luddites and the Swing rioters, the Newlyn fishermen had sought to interfere with the market rather than machinery. In the light of sweeping changes to the fishing industry and the onslaught of technological advancements, the people of Newlyn rightly feared for their jobs and their capacity to put food on the table at home. It is certainly true that in the years that followed the events of May 1896, the day of the smaller fishing units was marked. Even at the time, concern was aired over dwindling stocks of mackerel owing to the rapid mechanization of the industry. At the meeting held in the House of Commons, between the riot and the trials, where attempts at resolving the Sunday fishing issue were made, the chairman made a statement to the effect that there is not the slightest doubt that the way the East Coast boats fish was doing considerable injury to the trade of the native fishermen. Among the five members of parliament present were Thomas Bolitho MP, for the West country men, and H.S. Foster MP, for the East coast fishermen. A statement was read on behalf of the Cornishmen, it stated the belief that abstention from fishing on a Saturday and Sunday would be of pecuniary benefit to all concerned, owing to the fact that, 'there is no doubt that mackerel are becoming more scarce and are found at greater distance from the land and that the constant fishing prevents them from reaching their spawning grounds.'[10] The perils of over fishing were recognized at the time, but little if anything was done to protect fish stocks and the future of the fishing industry.

The 'industrialization' of fishing practices and a seemingly ever-expanding, insatiable market has given rise to concerns that are still echoed today. It also gave rise to a dispute in the North Atlantic, which came to a head in the late rioters and early 1970s. The Cod Wars, a food fight examined in the following chapter, highlighted concerns on behalf of the British fishing fleet over the loss of jobs and livelihoods. For the Icelandic fishermen, the fight was more to do with the sustainability of fish stocks themselves.

END NOTES

1. Jenkin, A.K. *Cornwall and its People,* p.80.
2. Ibid. p.94.
3. *The Cornishman* 21 May 1896.
4. Hansard 1896.
5. Reported in *The Cornishman* 18 June 1896.
6. *The Cornishman* 16 July 1896.
7. A line from *The Riot*, a play by Nick Darke
8. www.newlynarchive.org
9. Cited in *The Cornishman* 24 August 2006.
10. *The Cornishman* 18 June 1896.

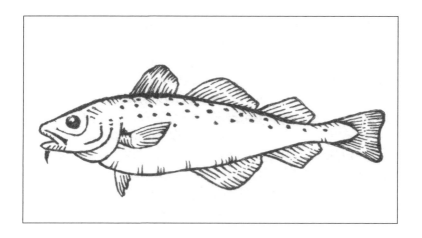

CHAPTER FIVE

PLENTY MORE FISH IN THE SEA

THE COD WARS

In a number of ways, the Cod Wars of the 1960s and 70s shared similarities with the 'Newlyn Fish Riots' of the previous century. In both disputes, technological advancements had lead to outlanders encroaching on others' territory. There were deep concerns for the viability of fish populations amongst the locals, livelihoods and local pride were at stake. This was a food fight which was to have lasting and significant consequences for the British fishing industry, as well as one which marked the beginnings of modern day concerns with the levels of fish stocks in British waters. The Cod Wars, of course, were fought hundreds of miles beyond British shores, and effectively began once Iceland gained independence from Denmark in 1944. Though the headlines weren't made until some three decades later, this was none the less a struggle which reflected the determination of a newly independent country to assert its own authority over its fishing grounds. From this perspective, the Cod Wars can be seen as a battle against the incremental enclosure of the seas, and perhaps marks the first time the British government chose to throw its lot in with the working man's efforts at combating enclosure.

In 1822, at the North Sea Fisheries Convention held in The Hague, Britain, Germany, the Netherlands, France and Denmark signed an agreement which established a three mile fishing limit around their shores. In 1901, a British and Danish convention declared that a three mile limit would also be applied to the territories of Greenland, the Faroe Islands and Iceland. Up to this point, the fishing fleets of many north European countries had landed catches almost within a stones throw of the Icelandic coast. The invention of the steam trawler had meant that those catches were becoming larger and larger, placing greater strains on the viability of fish stocks. The advent of the First World War meant that many of the British trawlers were commandeered by the Royal Navy and were adapted to provide gun boats offering protection around the waters closer to home. A similar approach was adopted during the Second World War as many boats were needed to protect the trans-atlantic convoys against the threat of German 'U Boats'. In 1949, having gained its independence just five years previously, Iceland served a two year notice of her intention to abrogate the British/Danish convention and extend the three mile fishing limit to four miles. By 1958, that limit had been extended to twelve miles. The threat to the British fishing fleet had begun.

Whilst other north European governments, Spain, France, Germany, Belgium, Denmark and the Netherlands, by and large complied with the new twelve mile limit, British trawlers, enjoying the protection of the Royal Navy, continued their fishing habits of years gone by. It was not until 1961 that the UK government recognized the twelve mile exclusion zone. The British were given a three year exception by Iceland, which permitted fishing within Icelandic waters, but at the same time, the Icelandic government declared its intentions of further extending its fishing limits in the future. In 1972, a new left-wing government in Iceland upped the exclusion zone to fifty miles, and it was this that sounded the death knell for the British distant water fishing fleet, though the final demise was not to come until some four years later.

Both Britain and Germany objected most strongly to the new 50 mile fishing limit off the Icelandic coast. The International Court of Law in the Hague upheld the British claim, but Iceland refused to recognize the findings of the court. Iceland maintained that it would protect its waters with its small fleet of coastguard vessels and its handful of naval gunboats. Despite warnings that the Icelanders would cut the trawl nets of any ships found fishing inside the exclusion zone, fishing boats from Grimsby, Hull, Aberdeen, Fleetwood and other British ports set sail to the old fishing grounds. Sixty British trawlers were to loose their nets during this period, forcing the skippers of those ships to return to their home ports for repairs and replacements. In the first instance, the British authorities at the time sent a number of ocean-going tug boats to offer protection to the fishing fleet. Tugboat skipper Norman Storey recounts the initial dismay of the trawler captains on hearing the news that no naval gun boats were to escort them. In his memoir of his role in the Cod Wars, Storey records the heroic efforts of the tug masters in protecting the trawlers. Storey's account brings a personal element to the tale, and paints an initial picture of a game of 'cat and mouse' played out between the fishermen and the Icelandic coastguard. Storey recounts the use of colourful language filling the VHF airwaves as the coastguard instructed the trawlers to haul their nets. A standard response from the British fleet ran along the lines of, 'my government say we are in international waters and I have a living to make and I must carry on fishing'. On other occasions, skippers simply jammed the airwaves, playing recordings of 'Rule Britannia', in breach of international radio convention. As incidences of trawl cutting and collisions between tugs and the Icelandic boats increased, the British government, once again, sent a number of frigates to protect domestic interests. Meanwhile, peace talks held in London were making little progress.

During the previous engagement during the 1960s, the Royal Navy had insisted on the fishing fleet remaining together, offering protection as the British trawlers fished within a designated pattern. Whilst this had made the job of the navy a little easier in terms of protecting the fleet, the fishermen suffered with poor catches. By the time of the second Cod War, the British skippers were much less prepared to listen to the requests of the naval officers. The fishing was better for all if the fleet went their own separate ways. Storey recounts tales recalling how each time a naval frigate retired to the Royal Navy Auxillary for refuelling, the trawler fleet would scatter. Tasked with staying with the fishing fleet, tug master Storey also describes the difficulties of working at sea in terrible weather conditions; in dense fog and using the radar, Storey drew his tug, the Lloydsman, close to what he assumed were a number of British trawlers working the fishing grounds together. Once the fog had cleared, however, it transpired that he had just spent several hours guarding an Icelandic fishing team. While effectively 'at war' on the high seas, both sides displayed a degree of camaraderie in searching for an Icelandic trawler reported missing in 1973. On another occasion, an English fisherman relayed a message to his brother on another boat in the area. He wished to send flowers to his wife on their wedding anniversary and could the brother help? The message went out on the VHF radio 'fishing channel' and on return home some time later he found that his wife had received no less than fourteen bunches of flowers, together with an equal number of loving messages of endearment!

Despite the bonhomie amongst the British fishermen, and a degree of professional respect between the Icelanders and the British fleet, the Cod Wars were fraught with danger. The close-quarter manoeuvres in rough seas, as Icelandic captains moved in to cut trawl nets, meant that collisions were common, and on occasion deliberate. The skippers of the tug boats offering protection, were a little more audacious than those of the Royal Navy, and this was recognized by some of the British fishermen. Hull skipper, Richard Taylor remarked on how it were as though the 'Icelandics were playing football on their own ground, they knew where the fish stocks were likely to be. The British Naval Captains on the other hand just knew how to pass the port – very handy in a cod war!'[1] To be fair to the naval officers, they were under orders at the time to avoid collision and so the course of action available to the captains was less than that of the unrestricted tug boat captains such as Norman Storey.

The fishing fleet had taken the precaution of painting over the names and numbers of their ships, in a bid to confuse the Icelandic patrols, but this was to prove ineffective as practically all of the British boats were familiar to the Icelandic authorities, having fished in their waters for many years. One of the key roles played by the Royal Navy was to alert the fishing fleet as to the whereabouts of the Icelandic gunboats, which were armed with the dreaded trawl cutters. Unbeknown to the British, the Icelandic captains had taken to recording the messages broadcast by the Royal Navy, stating positions of the gun boats. These would then be played over the airwaves a couple of days later, giving rise to much confusion. Once the navy began broadcasting pleas for the fishing fleet to ignore such messages, then the Icelanders would record and broadcast those too.

In 1974, Britain finally came to accept the 50 mile limit in return for a 2 year agreement, in which some 139 registered British trawlers were allowed to fish in restricted waters and limited a catch of up to 130,000 tons of fish. The following year, however, the Icelandic government once again extended the fishing limit, this time to 200 miles off the coast. Once again, naval frigates and tugs returned to the seas off the Icelandic coast to protect the interests of the British fleet. Relations between the two governments were so strained, that in February 1976, Iceland broke off all diplomatic relations with Britain.

In many ways, the Icelandic government were holding all the cards. Not only were they, as a country, asserting their rights to fish beyond the continental shelf, but they were stating the need to protect the breeding grounds and viability of the cod stocks in the North Atlantic. So the cod war was a food fight, fought not only in an attempt to protect the livelihoods of the fishermen involved (both British and Icelandic), but the welfare of the cod population was at stake too. Concerns over the levels of fish stocks have been voiced, predominantly by fishermen themselves, for many years. These concerns were to re-emerge in the twenty-first century and brought with them the opportunity for much broader based participation in a food fight which would have far-reaching consequences across Europe. The campaign led by food writer and broadcaster, Hugh Fearnley -Whittingstall, known initially as 'Hugh's Fish Fight' and later simply as 'Fish Fight', began in 2010. This campaign will be examined in a later chapter.

In 1976, NATO called for a meeting between the foreign ministers of the United Kingdom and Iceland and the matter was finally settled on 31 May. Britain had in effect lost the Cod War. Tom Nielson of the British Trawler Owners Federation stated in an interview with the Icelandic press that, 'you have won a great victory, and that I don't want to take away. The sad thing is that you've put a hell of a lot of hard working and good fishermen out of work.'[2] The impact on the British fishing fleet and industry as a whole is still felt today. Although Britain also extended her fishing limits to two hundred miles in 1976, the end of the cod wars marked the end of Britain's distant water fishing practices. Many of the trawlers were broken up after their final trip home.

Having gained its independence in 1944, Iceland and its nascent fishing industry had enjoyed a brief period of respite as British ships had been requisitioned by the Royal Navy for use while Britain was at war. Prior to that, between 1914 and 1918 Icelandic fishermen, then under Danish sovereignty, had witnessed a significant increase in fish stocks and corresponding catches in the absence of the British fishing fleet. The onset of war brought, for Iceland at least, a boon in the availability of food. In Britain it was a very different story.

END NOTES

1. Quoted in BBC TV documentary, *History of the Cod Wars*. Screened on BBC4 9 May 2010.
2. Ibid.

DEFENCE OF THE REALM.

MINISTRY OF FOOD

BREACHES OF THE RATIONING ORDER

The undermentioned convictions have been recently obtained:—

Court	Date	Nature of Offence	Result
HENDON	29th Aug 1918	Unlawfully obtaining and using ration books	3 Months Imprisonment
WEST HAM	29th Aug 1918	Being a retailer and failing to detach proper number of coupons	Fined £20
SMETHWICK	22nd July 1918	Obtaining meat in excess quantities	Fined £50 & £5 5s costs
OLD STREET	4th Sept. 1918	Being a retailer selling to unregistered customer	Fined £72 & £5 5s costs
OLD STREET	4th Sept. 1918	Not detaching sufficient coupons for meat sold	Fined £25 & £2 2s costs
CHESTER-LE-STREET	4th Sept. 1918	Being a retailer obtaining number of registered customers in excess of counterfoils deposited	Fined £50 & £3 3s costs
HIGH WYCOMBE	7th Sept. 1918	making false statement and application for and using ration books unlawfully	Fined £40 & £6 6s costs

Enforcement Branch, Local Authorities Division
MINISTRY OF FOOD

CHAPTER SIX

NOT ENOUGH TO GO ROUND

Rationing as Crowd Control in a Time of War

The sight of large crowds gathering in the streets and demanding food was a familiar one towards the end of the First World War, and were known as food queues. Whilst these gatherings were perhaps of a much more orderly nature than the full-on food riots which had occurred in previous centuries, government concern for potential unrest in the streets at home in a time of national crisis ran deep, and a system of rationing was developed to prevent the growth of food queues. Food queues in some areas of the country were so bad that men engaged in the manufacture of munitions were leaving work to take the places of their wives in the line for food. Serious and growing discontent was reported from all industrial districts of the country.[1]

That the advent of large queues in British towns and cities prompted and illustrated the need for a system of rationing is born out by newspaper reports at the time. Newspapers had begun to report the growth of the 'food queue' and its flashpoint potential. In December 1917, *The Times* reported that food queues were a growing concern, citing queues of up to 1,000, and in another case 3,000 strong as people waited to buy tea and margarine. By January of 1918, shortages of meat were the concern of the public, as well as to butchers themselves. William H. Beveridge in his treatise on British Food Control (1928) cites queues of butchers at Smithfield market (wholesalers) running up to 500 long. The need for a national scheme of rationing was apparent and on Sunday 14 July 1918, Britain was subject to a rationing scheme, which was to last into the post war years.

Rationing is a military term and carries with it connotations of equality and discipline, as a limited supply of goods is divided among those who need them. Rationing in the United Kingdom began in 1917, in part, as a result of the threat to shipping, brought about by the success of German submarine warfare. This was seen to lead to a depletion of food supplies available to the public at home, as well as to serving soldiers abroad. Scenes of virtual panic set in as the government came to realize that stocks of certain foodstuffs had dwindled to just three or four weeks supply. Sugar was the first commodity to be rationed, as the main source of Britain's sugar came through Austria-Hungary, and that supply chain had dried up more or less at the outbreak of the war. Sugar was rationed via a system which developed as the government at the time introduced the principle of the 'datum period', whereby wholesalers were limited to a percentage of the amount of sugar they sold in 1915 (a period before the threat to supply). Limiting supply to wholesalers, however, did not directly limit the amount of sugar available to individuals, as retailers were unable to prevent individual consumers from visiting a number of shops to purchase sugar, thus adding to the problem of scarcity. By spring of 1918, the rationing system had developed further, as the government introduced a 'second currency', the ration ticket, which was needed to authorize the purchase of selected foodstuffs in specific quantities. This was a much more effective means of tackling the problem of demand outstripping supply, as the total number of tickets issued could be adjusted in line with the supplies available. The system was further honed by tying individual customers to particular retailers and ensuring that those retailers were in turn supplied with enough provisions to meet the demands of their customers.

Rationing is arguably the ultimate form of crowd control in times of scarcity. Through the compulsory introduction of the notion of a 'fair share', potential fights over dwindling supplies are, in theory at least, avoided. Towards the end of the First World War it was applied in Britain for the first time. In December of 1916, Lord Devonport took office as Britain's first Minister for Food Control. Throughout the duration of the war, a total of four Food Controllers held office. Lord Rhonda succeeded Devonport in 1917, followed by J.R. Clynes in 1918, George Roberts in 1919, and Charles McCurdy in 1920. McCurdy was the last Food Controller during this period, and in 1921 the post was abandoned.

In June 1917, Food Control Committees were established in over 2,000 districts of the country. Householders were obliged to register with the Food Office, detailing the names, ages and occupations of all those living at every address in the country.

In what is perhaps one of the earliest published (1918) books dealing with the subject of rationing, A.J. Philip, a member of the Gravesend Food Control Committee at the time, and the first of the food committees to introduce sugar rationing, put forward the idea that it was the queue that caused the introduction of the rationing scheme in the first place. Philip held that, queues proved themselves the cause of a 'cycle of evil', in that not only did the people endeavour to obtain more than they desired, contributing to scarcity and feeding the 'cycle', they showed up ever more early each day, rendering it more and more difficult for the shopkeeper to cope. His somewhat less than clement observation appears to lay the blame for food queues firmly at the feet of the female population: 'Worth considering was that of the pleasure many women took in finding in the queue, or the professed need to stand in a queue, an opportunity for gossip' he goes on to claim that in spending time standing in a queue, the woman 'neglected her housework and scamped the cooking, to the detriment of the health and happiness of her home.'[2]

It can only be a delicious coincidence that rationing in Britain, developed in part at least as a means of heading off food riots, was first introduced in the district of Gravesend. At that time, Gravesend was the point from which, having been held aboard the prison hulks, so many people convicted of participating in food riots during the previous century were transported as punishment for their crimes.

At the time, great efforts were made to demonstrate that this was a rationing scheme which applied equally to every citizen in the country, regardless of their position. To re-iterate this, reproductions of the King's own ration books were presented in newspapers for all to see. The 'all in this together' approach, then as much as now, however, would not be sufficient to ensure that rules weren't bent. The national rationing scheme was backed up with strict laws of enforcement. The number of prosecutions against those seeking to take advantage of the rationing system, in particular against shopkeepers caught selling items above the maximum upper price limit (which seemed to make up the highest number of cases for prosecution) were significant in the first full year of rationing.

It became illegal to hoard or to waste food. A woman in Wales was fined £20 for feeding meat to a St. Bernard dog, an unfortunate furnace man was fined £10 for throwing his chips into the fire, and following a tiff with her husband, a woman was fined £5 for burning stale bread on the lawn. In what must have been a less than pleasant investigation which involved a food executive officer and a policeman picking out rock cakes from a tub of pig swill and tasting them (to no ill effect), a Lincolnshire farmer was fined £10 for wasting human food. This seemed a particularly harsh prosecution as the farmer had managed to buy a job lot of unwanted stale rock cakes from an Army canteen to feed his pigs. A Yorkshire farmer was imprisoned for three months for feeding bread to his cows.[3] Successful prosecutions were reported regularly in the National Food Journal (published by the Ministry of Food) and the ethos of rationing as a great leveller was truly tested, as those prosecuted for hoarding food, as opposed to wasting it, did not appear to come from the working classes amongst the populace.

Beveridge details an almost comical range of upper class chicanery; a best selling author fined £50, an earl's daughter fined £80, a member of the House of Commons, fined £400 and hundreds of pounds of food confiscated, a vicar whose collar was felt having been caught with a bag of sugar in his broken-down car as the police came to his aid, a baronet who managed to wriggle out of prosecution on the grounds that tea was not classed as food (it yields no calories). The extent of hoarding in 1918 was such that, in a manner similar to which modern police forces hold gun and knife amnesties in a bid to render the streets a safer place, Food Control Agencies were given to holding 'Conscience Week' in February of that year, whereby food surrendered was sold, and half the proceeds of the sale would go to the person surrendering. Those who did not place trust in the promised clemency simply abandoned their hoards anonymously on municipal doorsteps.

The number of prosecutions brought about under the Food Control Orders dropped from 28,657 in 1918 to 21,698 in 1919. From these figures, it appears that people either fell in line with the rationing system pretty quickly, or, and perhaps more likely, figured out how to play the game without getting caught. It should also be said, of course, that the war was by then over and the future appeared a little brighter. The less diligent black marketeers, however, were up against a system which managed to deliver a high percentage of successful prosecutions. Out of 50,355 prosecutions in 1918 and 1919, roughly 92% of those carried convictions, including prison sentences and fines.[4]

Despite the unpopularity of the rationing system, it did serve to banish the food queue and dispel the feeling of panic and anxiety among much of the food buying population of the country. The feelings of panic, however, were soon to return to the British public, as in the immediate post-war period food prices began to climb rapidly. This first period of food rationing, like the one that followed twenty years later outlasted the war itself, much to the dismay of the British public. Immediate relief from rationing came in the form of easing restrictions on the use of imported flour:

the right to make cakes and pastries of every kind and to cover them with sugar or chocolate or both was restored to Britons on the 7th December 1918, as was the right to eat an unlimited quantity of these or other cakes at afternoon tea.[5]

Rations for beef, mutton and veal were increased following the Armistice, and continued into 1919, but pork, poultry and game were taken out of rationing a few short weeks after the restrictions on flour were lifted.

The decontrol of food after the First World War presented a number of problems. The debate over premature demobilization was muted in parliament, and opinions on the speed at which the Ministry of Food and food control in general ought be abolished, swung to and fro. While the debate raged, prices were still rising, and the government sought to intervene by tackling the problem of food supply. Price rises were actually swaying public opinion in favour of the continuation of food control measures and this change in trend was presented by the Consumer Council. As a result, in July 1919, George Roberts, the Food Controller at the time, announced to the House of Commons that the Ministry of Food would continue with full powers for the foreseeable future and that meat, butter, bacon, eggs, milk, bread, margarine and fish would remain under control. Control extended to tackling issues of supply rather than trying to restrict consumption with a revival of the coupon system.[6]

The first period of rationing in Britain ended in 1920, and amid claims of rationing having introduced an improved diet to the British public, Beveridge observed that:

the main lesson in British food control is that State trading in food is practicable and in time of prolonged shortage is necessary. It is within the wit of man to find an alternative to competitive private enterprise with market prices as a means of obtaining and distributing food, to replace economic by human laws, to substitute managed for automatic provisioning of the people. The British people in every part of Britain were fed during the war without interruption. Moreover, they were fed far more cheaply and fairly than they could have been fed by private enterprise. Private traders could not and would not, after the submarine war began in earnest, have taken the risks essential to secure continuity of sufficient supplies.[7]

With these words, Beveridge captured a dilemma which was to plague the government in its deliberations over whether or not to discontinue rationing. The benefits of rationing, in terms of distribution, availability and price to the consumer were all there to be seen as government took direct control over agricultural production. On the other hand, the cost of subsidies promised and paid to farmers during this period proved of enormous concern to the exchequer, and were instrumental in the government at the time relinquishing control and reverting to a *laissez faire* approach such as that which was in place before the war.

The period of depression and the series of hunger marches in the 1920s and throughout the 1930s, which took place in a post-rationing period, appear to lend credence to Beveridge's claims, in that once state control of food was relinquished to the free market after 1920, the larders of the working classes appeared bare once more.

With the post-war boom in decline, unemployment in 1920 had risen to some 6%. The 'land fit for heroes' failed to materialize and this lead to widespread agitation. The first national march of this period took place in 1922, with marchers from Scotland being joined by workers form the North East, Liverpool and the Midlands. Contingents from Wales and the South West also joined the procession. Marching an average of twelve miles per day, and ending in London, this was a well organized demonstration of protest. The rules of the march were printed in the programme, they stipulated the need for discipline and obedience to the marshals' instructions. Each contingent must have its own banner showing the name of the town. The loaves on sticks and slogans of 'bread or blood' may have been replaced with colourful emblems of trade union movements and friendly societies, but the symbolism was not lost on the authorities. Contingents organized finance subcommittees in order to deal with donations received along the route. Some 20,000 people convened for a rally in Hyde Park to meet the marchers as they arrived. The then Prime Minister Bonar Law refused to meet with the marchers. Hunger marches were common in the inter-war period, with others taking place in 1927, 1930, 1932, 1934 and the famous 'Jarrow Crusade' in 1936. The hunger march of 1932 was the largest of these demonstrations. Organized by the National Unemployed Workers Movement (NUWM), those marching were calling for employment and carried a petition against the use of means testing as a gatekeeper to poor relief. Marching beneath banners proclaiming, 'We Refuse to Starve in Silence' (a motif which bares a striking resemblance to the old cry of 'we'd rather be hanged than starve to death'), and 'End the Means Test Now', the crowd of some 1,500 marchers arrived at Hyde Park on the 27 October. Numbers swelled as some 100,000 local supporters showed up to voice their concerns. Violence broke out at the closing rally in Hyde Park as the government refused to accept the petition which the marchers had carried, and the ranks of some 2,000 police officers sought to break up the rally. The individual hunger marches could claim no significant concessions from governments at the time, but collectively they certainly served to reiterate the conditions under which the poor working classes were living in some parts of the country. It could be argued that they were to inform the shape of the future welfare state, in that the hunger marchers between them, together with the voices of support they found along their routes, put forward the notion of 'welfare' as a common benefit.

While the hungry and unemployed marched the length and breadth of the country in their tens of thousands, the government set up The National Mark Movement in 1928. Building on the success of increasing domestic yields during the First World War, the National Mark was established with a view to the standardization of quality in food production. Home grown produce was subject to grading in terms of the quality of the product. A booklet produced by the Ministry of Agriculture and Fisheries, printed in 1935, assured housewives that foodstuffs that bore the National Mark (an emblem depicting the outline of England and Wales with a circular Union Jack at its centre) were of the utmost quality and were domestically produced. 'Don't shop in the dark, look for the National Mark', was the bold advice given in the booklet, which contained upwards of 100 recipes. Ambrose Heath wrote in the first chapter:

> In National Mark beef you have the same high quality all through; and if you want your Sunday joint to cost you less, you might well try buying some of the cheaper cuts during the week.[8]

It seems incredible to think that the government was concerned with standardizing quality, and offering options on the 'Sunday roast', as tens of thousands of hungry citizens marched on London. Less than five years later, however, Britain was once again at war and food production and distribution was once more the job of the government.

The start of the Second World War introduced a food fight on a much larger global scale. Hitler's designs on securing supplies of Ukrainian grain, and his desire to control the 'bread basket' of Europe through the agrarian policy of the Nazi regime, ushered in a period during which food once again became a weapon of war. By 1941, Lord Woolton the Minister for Food declared to the nation:

> This is a food war. Every extra row of vegetables in allotments saves shipping. The battle on the kitchen front cannot be won without help from the kitchen garden.[9]

The organization of food control measures, and the re-introduction of rationing in Britain was in many respects a deal easier than it had been in 1918. The expansion of domestic agricultural output during the latter part of the First World War meant that Britain was slightly less dependent on imported food. A rapid programme of mechanization and a campaign to plough pasture and turn it into arable land, together with the efforts of the Women's Land Army increased Britain's output and cut back on valuable shipping space.

British farming underwent great change during this period as

County War Agricultural Executive Committees (War Ags) were convened with sweeping powers including the authority to take possession of land, to terminate tenancies and to direct what crops were grown. In 1941, the War Ags were directed by the Ministry of Agriculture and Fisheries to conduct a Farm Survey of Britain. All farms over five acres were to be included in the survey, which established the tenure, land condition, water supplies, fertility and productivity of every farm in the country. In cases where the land was deemed derelict, or farms were regarded as grossly inefficient, the land could be taken under the control of the executive committees. It was actions such as these that were to have a lasting effect on food production in this country, and one which informs the shape of the food chain today.

By 1939 the science of nutrition had developed to such an extent that nutritionalists suddenly held sway in positions of power both within government and the military and were able to exert a level of influence on food policies.[10] A key player in formulating Britain's new rationing policies was Jack Drummond, professor of Biochemistry at University College London. Professor Drummond was a nutritionist, with a keen interest in food at a personal level. He was an early member of the Food and Wine Society, founded by André Simon in 1933, and a pioneer in the field of nutritional studies. His only book, *The Englishman's Food* – five centuries of English diet, was published before the war in 1939. It presented an analysis of diet in England, paying careful attention to the relationship between health and diet among ordinary working people as well as looking at the food of the wealthy classes. Drummond also sheds light in his book on the diets of children in schools, soldiers and inmates. Highlighting the rise of the science of nutrition, he put forward recommended diets for optimal health as well as advice on the preservation of food. It was perhaps the publication of this book, which saw Drummond appointed to the post of Scientific Advisor to the Ministry of Food in 1940. Professor Drummond recognized the need to educate the public in nutritional matters and via the Food Advice Division of the Ministry of Food he was able to direct a number of successful programmes and campaigns, which not only left the British public better informed, but also raised standards of cooking in domestic kitchens; 'dig for Victory', 'thoughtful shopping saves shipping', 'food or munitions, eat potatoes instead' were all popular slogans, posters and leaflets which emanated form Jack Drummond's department during the war and helped raise nutritional knowledge among those on the home front. He was knighted in 1944, and after the war took a position as research director at Boots Pure Drug Company. Sadly, Drummond, his wife, and his ten-year-old daughter were murdered, amid tragic circumstances, while on holiday in France in 1952.

A number of lessons about food control measures had been learned during the previous war. The run-up to rationing in 1940 had begun four years earlier, when the government set up the Food Defence Planning Department under the Board of Trade. It was this department, which morphed into the new Ministry of Food on the outbreak of war in 1939.

The rationing system in 1941 was further developed to include a points rationing scheme. The points system applied to foods of value, but which were not essential to the basic diet and very short in supply (and therefore could not be rationed across the board). Items such as tinned meat, fish and fruit were subject to the points system, whereby householders were awarded a number of 'points' each week, and could 'spend' these points as they wished. The items under this system carried a monetary value as well as a points value. The government was able to adjust the value of points according to which items were in supply at the time, and that way 'steer' the public into buying specific foodstuffs.

The Food Control Committees, convened during the First World War, were reinstated, and the wily British public once more sought to put food on the table in times of austerity. Again, the ethos of collective hardship prevailed, however, as under the previous regime of rationing, there were those who sought to fight against the rules, and who found new ways of benefitting from the rationing system, and providing for their families at home. In less than six months, from the outbreak of war to the end of March the following year, a total of thirty-five retailers were fined for overcharging for potatoes and one hundred and ninety were fined for overcharging for other foodstuffs. Even well established larger stores, including Sainsbury's, Woolworths, and D.H. Evans fell foul of the new laws and faced prosecution in the courts. The number of prosecutions under the various Food Control Acts remained consistent with the numbers of those brought to justice 20 years previously; in the period October 1940 to 30 September 1941, there were a total of 25,219 prosecutions, of which 23,704 were successful.[11] It is perhaps of little surprise that, as well as members of the general public, a number of those who faced prosecution under the Control of Food Act were actually members of food control committees and persons placed in a position of responsibility under the rationing laws. In 1941, a member of the Richmond Food Control Committee, himself the manager of a butchers shop, was convicted of attempting to supply unlawfully seven joints of meat to his own household. He was fined £50 and ordered to pay fifteen guineas in costs. A Leonard D. Blake of the Barking Food Control Office, together with eight other men and a woman were all charged with conspiring to contravene the provisions of the sugar control order (1940), as many tons of sugar were obtained improperly and sold by the defendants.

Rather than being 'all in it together', from these figures it appears that a significant proportion of the population were all 'at it together'. As well as out and out corruption, the ingenious British public found a number of ways to circumvent regulations under food control, whether to make a few quid on the side or to get by in times or severe hardship. What is clear is that the role of the State altered significantly in order to bring in rationing and head off any potential unrest sparked by scarcity of food supplies. It is also of interest that, despite the government's active attempts to ensure that everyone was fed, individuals still sought to further their own interests.

In Britain, the modern image of the wartime black marketeer is conjured in one of two stereotypes. This is largely due to the highly popular television series, *Dad's Army* which aired on the BBC between the late 1960s through to 1977. *Dad's Army* depicted the hapless exploits of a company of aged Home Guard volunteers based in the fictional village of Warmington-on-Sea during the Second World War. Among the ranks of the Warmington volunteers were a corporal Jones and a private Walker. Jones was the elderly village butcher who was happy to offer his regular customers 'a little something under the counter' in the form of an extra sausage or a lamb chop or two. Private Walker, on the other hand, was a younger man, a loveable rogue who offered a fine line of contraband tobacco and ladies nylons. Once again, the Black Market was to play a role in the food supply of a nation at war, but the likes of Private Walker, and other spivs and racketeers like him were not seen as affable 'Jack-the-lad' characters at the time. Prosecutions soared and the image of the black marketeer was portrayed as that of a traitor. Prosecutors and magistrates looked upon those accused as saboteurs or robbers of the nation's food. In 1941, the Secretary of the London Chamber of Commerce warned the government of the dangers of food racketeers becoming 'like gangsters in the USA' unless checked. But the role of the Black Market was there to be played out; even the Ministry of Food was implicated in double dealing after salvaging goods from warehouses and docks damaged during the blitz and channelling it back on to the streets via the underground network of dodgy dealers and organized crime, which seemed to have a more extensive and efficient distribution network. In Liverpool in 1941, in response to complaints by the public, a local butcher, William Alfred Eales, was investigated by CID and placed under arrest. Under questioning, Eales revealed his co-conspirators, one of whom was a Donald Shaw, a Ministry of Food supervisor for meat distribution at Warrington. Both Eales and Shaw, together with four others were imprisoned for their part in the racket.[12]

The struggle to make do with dwindling resources continued as the war progressed, and the efforts required to put a meal on the table, became harder. In this respect, the nature of the food fight also changed. For those on the Home Front, the food fight became a fight with food, a fight to make what little ingredients there were available go further, and to replicate menus and meals that had been enjoyed before the war, when fats, eggs and flour were in abundance. Colquhoun describes cooks as 'kitchen warriors' employing ever more resourceful methods to eek out the ration. Fat skimmed from soups and stews was used in cake making, butter papers hoarded to grease tins, eggs were 'pickled' so they could be kept longer in solutions of isinglass kept in zinc buckets. Ingenuity and guile were used to their full extent in the struggle, as the Minister of Food Lord Woolton, lent his name to a brave attempt at a sumptuous meal of an assortment of root vegetables, tucked up beneath a blanket of 'potato' pastry. 'Woolton Pie' was one of a host of ersatz, make-do dishes. Where the real thing had once graced the table, crafty alternatives which stretched the imagination way beyond any traditional menu were found in a staggering array of 'mock' alternatives; 'mock crab', 'mock cream', 'mock fishcakes', 'mock apricot tart', where sliced carrots took the place of apricots, all took culinary improvization to new levels.

Perhaps due to an over generous helping of nostalgia (an ingredient which wasn't on ration at the time) this period of culinary craftwork is often viewed or portrayed today as a period when the nation struggled together to ward off food poverty. The government at the time went to great lengths to ensure that people didn't go hungry. Anthropomorphic vegetables appeared on billboard and poster campaigns, as Potato Pete and Doctor Carrot sought to reiterate the importance of nutrition in the diet. The Buggins Family, from the popular long-running radio show of the same name, was recruited to the daily broadcast of 'Kitchen Front' on the BBC Home Service. 'Grandma Buggins' offered regular sound advice to millions of listeners through her curmudgeonly diktats on food and sensible eating. Other contemporary popular figures were enrolled in a more formal capacity; Dame Marguerite Patten presented a regular programme of recipes for the kitchen warriors struggling to make do with a depleted larder. As the war pressed on and large numbers of people were bombed out of their homes, the government set up a number of community feeding sentries, or British Restaurants, as they were more popularly known. These provided a centre where people could gather to eat a square meal once a day at affordable prices.

The advent of two world wars marked a period where collective action was once again used as a means of securing a lasting supply of food. In this particular case, that action was sanctioned on a national level and directed by the government at the time. In this respect, I would argue that the whole country can be seen as being engaged in a collective food struggle, an effort to put food on the table, and one in which the struggle was seen as working for a common good at a time of national crisis. Perhaps unsurprizingly, there were of course those engaged in practises seeking to further their own circumstances. The black marketeers, while to a degree fulfilling a role, or a gap in the market left open by the rationing system, were motivated largely by their own desire for riches, rather than any philanthropic tendencies. As with riots which took place in previous centuries, there were individuals who sought to gain from the proceedings. In contrast to the national collectivism prevalent during the times of conflict, what is particularly striking is the period between the wars, where the working classes were once again left to their own devices, many driven to participating in vast organized hunger marches as a means of getting their point across. The days of food riots at the butter cross, or in the market square were long gone. Two world wars had shown the value in working collectively to put food on the table. Not only that, by the end of the Second World War, the structure of the food chain, or the food system, had altered as the mass production of food on a commercial level was seen as the best way of feeding a nation. This change was to alter the nature of food riots which followed.

END NOTES

1. Beveridge, W.H. *British Food Control*, p.196.
2. Philip, A.J. *Rations, Rationing and Food Control*, p.9.
3. Beveridge, W.H. *British Food Control*, p.238.
4. Ibid. p.236.
5. Ibid. p.269.
6. Hansard 14 July 1919.
7. Beveridge, W.H. *British Food Control*, p.337/338.

8. National Mark recipe book, Issued by Ministry of Agriculture & Fisheries, 1935.

9. Cited: http://www.carrotmuseum.co.uk/history4.html#disney

10. Collingham, L. *The Taste of War*, p.10.

11. Hansard, October 1941.

12. Thomas, D. *An Underworld at War*, p.134.

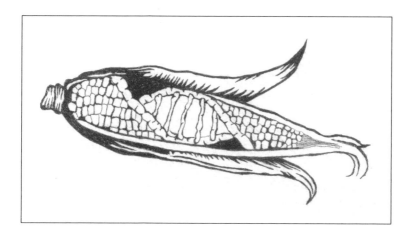

CHAPTER SEVEN

THE TIMES THEY ARE A' CHANGING

The Development of the Modern Food System and the Growing Battle for 'Food Security'

On a scorching day in the middle of July 1999, a ghost army lined up on the edge of a field in the agricultural heart of Oxfordshire. For a moment, no one spoke or stirred. The pennants snapped and slackened in the wind, and the five hundred revenant warriors, white suited, white cowled, white masked, rippled, broke and reunited in the heat haze without stirring a limb. Someone somewhere along the line must have shouted, for all at once the horde surged forward, half walking, half running, banners streaming, sticks raised, yelling and cheering. The handful of black-clad men who opposed them – the infantry of the British Crown – gave way, and the army poured into the field. It marched for two hundred yards then stopped. No opposing force stood in its way: the ranked ghosts confronted an enemy even more spectral than themselves. They raised their sticks and struck, slashing not at the air in front of them, but at the ground beneath their feet. The battlefield was not merely the scene of combat, but the enemy itself.[1]

With these words, George Monbiot describes the destruction of one of Britain's first 'farm-scale' trials of genetically modified (GM) crops. The protests marked the beginning of a modern day food fight, one which has its roots firmly planted within an ideological debate, and which emerged from the realization of the benefits of mass food production towards the end of the Second World War. Hardly a riot as such, although had the authorities been present they might have claimed otherwise, as through the destruction of property, the actions of the protestors mimic the efforts of the Swing rioters of the early nineteenth century. It is the association of intellectual property and intellectual property rights that comes in tandem with genetic modification that present a challenge to the food fighters of today. Opponents to the use of GM face a formidable enemy, as they are often portrayed as taking food from the mouths of the hungry. As recently as October 2013, the then Environment Secretary, Owen Paterson, described non government organizations such as Greenpeace and Friends of the Earth that oppose GM technology as 'wicked' and 'casting a dark shadow over attempts to feed the world.'[2]

The advent of two world wars changed, forever, the way we think about feeding the planet. In the United Kingdom at least, as the government took over a number of 'inefficient' smaller farms in a drive to increase food production, a new era of farming began. The future of small-scale farming was limited. The shortages brought on by war reinforced the notion that 'big is beautiful' and paved the way for the large scale and corporate farming we know today. By the end of the Second World War, governments and scientists, including the unfortunate Professor Jack Drummond, had identified a new challenge; to ensure that agricultural productivity was able to keep in step with population growth and a dietary transition brought about by rising incomes in post war prosperity. Atlee and the Labour Party's post war manifesto, which implored voters to 'face the future', had claimed that 'people need food at prices they can afford to pay'. Food supplies were now, very much, the business of government. The shock Labour victory in the 1945 general election meant that many of the measures introduced during the war, free milk for mothers and children, work canteens and British restaurants would become part of the 'fixtures and fittings' of the country, driven now by an ideological verve, rather than a need to survive in times of war. The late 1940s witnessed the onset of the 'Green Revolution', which was clearly a reference to chlorophyll, rather than a moniker bearing the sustainable connotations of today's use of the word 'green'. In order to deliver on the promise of feeding the masses, the Green Revolution ushered in the broader mechanization and improved irrigation in farming. The number of tractors on British farms practically trebled in ten years, from 101,500 in 1942 to 324,960 in 1952. During this period, the use of nitrogen-based fertilizers and pesticides expanded greatly. This revolution did much to increase yields and gave rise to the flourishing of new agrochemical companies, such that between 1945 and 1960, worldwide sales of agrochemicals grew by 7% every year, and by the 1990s, the total world market in agrochemicals was worth more than $21 billion.

The way in which the Attlee government embraced new scientific discovery and its application to agriculture is not without its criticism. At the time, little concern was given to the potential harmful effects of the emerging new agrochemicals. Inefficient farms were threatened with state 'supervision', those that failed to adhere to the 'rules of good estate management and good husbandry' were likely to have their farms seized by the state. This mighty stick was wielded in chapter 48 of the 1947 Agriculture Act, giving the government power of compulsory purchase over farms in 'supervision' which were failing to show signs of improvement. In just four years between 1948 and 1952, some four thousand supervision orders were issued and more than two hundred and fifty farmers and landowners were dispossessed. 'Good husbandry', of course, included the use of many of the newly developed agrochemicals, in particular weed killers and pesticides.

In the face of such formidable weaponry as the 1947 Agriculture Act and the 1949 'Pest Control Act', together with the financial incentives offered by the Ministry of Agriculture, farmers and growers were left with little option but to embrace the new technologies. It marked a period in which the new chemical companies appeared to hold a deal of sway over the government, and one which appears to exist right up until today. In his 1987 volume, *The Politics of Food*, writer, editor and broadcaster, Geoffrey Cannon points out the links which remain between politicians on both sides of the house and the interests of the multinational companies which wield control over the food system today.

Those that opposed the emerging chemical onslaught of the land, particularly during the war years, were subject to ridicule and derision, but undeterred in their efforts. Lady Evelyn Balfour, niece of the former conservative Prime Minister Lord Arthur Balfour, had her heart set on a career as a farmer from an early age. With a degree in agriculture from Reading University, she set about her ambition and purchased a farm in Suffolk, where she pioneered a series of agricultural experiments. The Haughley Experiment was one of the first side-by-side trials established to draw comparisons between chemically based, and organic methods of farming. She published the initial results of her findings in 1943 in her best selling book *The Living Soil*. Concerned over soil erosion, the effect that the new agrochemicals might have on wildlife, and sceptical of the nutritional value of intensely farmed food, Balfour set about forming the Soil Association in 1946.

The Soil Association today campaigns vigorously against use of genetically modified (GM) crops. It continues to be one of the loudest anti-GM voices in the country, providing advice, technical support and knowledge to farmers, businesses and research institutions across the United Kingdom. It campaigns for healthy, humane and sustainable food, farming and land use in the UK, and remains firmly against the commercial planting of GM crops in the UK, as well as the use of GM ingredients in human and animal food. The Soil Association has arguably taken Eve Balfour's original ideas out of the field and planted them in the homes, gardens, allotments, schools and minds of tens of thousands of people over the intervening years. The educational role of the Soil Association has grown as the organization has developed. Its Food for Life Partnership, for example, is designed to give children a broad food education, based not just on healthy eating, but on understanding where food comes from and how it is produced.

Broad based public support for organizations like the Soil Association didn't emerge until many years after they were established, and even then this support was slow in building. The environmental impact of the 'Green Revolution' was not widely recognized, but this began to change during the 1960s. Writing in America during the late 1950s, marine biologist, writer and ecologist, Rachel Carson, began to highlight the plight of wildlife, and in particular birds, which were dying in large numbers in the fields and hedgerows of American farms, as a direct result of the over enthusiastic use of pesticides on crops. Carson's ground breaking book *Silent Spring*, which was first published in 1962, captured the attention of a broader public, both in America and Europe, and arguably laid the foundations for a resurgence in environmental movements across the world, as she highlighted the dangers of pesticide poisoning, not just to wildlife, but also the risk to humans through consumption down the food chain:

> The whole problem of pesticide poisoning is enormously complicated by the fact that the human being, unlike a laboratory animal living under rigidly controlled conditions, is never exposed to one chemical alone. Between the major groups of insecticides, and between them and other chemicals, there are interactions that have serious potentials. Whether released into soil or water or man's blood, these unrelated chemicals do not remain segregated; there are mysterious and unseen changes by which one alters the power of another for harm.[3]

Carson's observations, as well as her extraordinary capacity to present frightening, and to put it mildly, downright depressing, news in such readable terms, had an impact almost as it ran off the publisher's presses. In England, she noted, the problems arose from treating seed with insecticide before sewing, particularly after chemicals designed to kill soil dwelling insects were added to seed stock. The British government was quick to act, but only once word found its way to the House of Lords. Many members of the Upper House, as landowners themselves, were being advized by gamekeepers of the devastation among game birds and other wildlife on their country estates. In 1961, a House of Commons Select Committee was convened to investigate the matter. In what must have been a ground breaking and radical approach to product development, the Committee recommended controls and field tests on new chemicals before being deployed. The fact that new chemicals and man made fertilizers were being used without regard to potential environmental consequences was picked up by a broader public.

The impact of *Silent Spring* brought about a closer inspection and greater consideration on behalf of many governments as to what was considered good estate management and good husbandry. It helped raise the issue of sustainability and prepared a battlefield for a food fight, which would not only operate in a global capacity, but one that would continue to develop in other directions, opening up a number of new fronts with potential for 'conflict'. Ever increasing scientific and technological developments have continued to shift the locus of struggle.

If the food fight of the 1960s and 70s, in this country at least, could be described along the lines of a simple rift between the 'Green Revolutionaries' and those promoting organic farming, with the former reigning supreme, then by the late twentieth century, a number of new fronts had opened up. The struggle for 'food security' is the food fight for the modern age. Food security in this context has little or nothing to do with the integrity or the provenance of food, rather it focuses around the availability of food. Food security is as much an individual concern as it is global. The very term itself seems loaded. At the individual and family level in Britain, food security, or the lack of it, is frequently in the news and is perhaps best illustrated by the growing use of food banks in this country.

The broad concept of 'food security', particularly on a national and global level, was perhaps first grasped by the public towards the end of the first World War, when Britain was struggling to feed itself in the face of the German submarine attacks on Atlantic food convoys. Even today, Britain imports up to 40% of the food we eat. Today, the concept of food security is presented as a global concern, and one which comes pre-packed with its own ideological battleground. Often portrayed as a 'struggle to feed the world' in the face of rapid population growth, diminishing land supplies and climate change, the 'problem' of food security appears to be one of volume and quantity, i.e. the need to produce more food in order that all at the table will have something to eat. Within the past decade, 'food security' has become the 'mantra du jour'. It appears to have abrogated the pledge to 'end world hunger', which emerged with the setting-up of the World Food Programme in 1961. The term 'food security' appeals to the language of our age, it carries an inherent connotation. It's one of those terms of reference that we all think we understand. A bit like '9/11', 'the war on terror', 'terrorist', or even those dreaded words, 'health and safety', the term brings with it an air of legitimacy and an assumed compliance or understanding. Terms like these are often presented and bandied about in the media to the extent that they become familiar household words, which are seldom explored beyond a nod of recognition. The term was defined at the World Food Summit in 1996 as being, 'when all people at all times have access to sufficient, safe, nutritious food to maintain a healthy and active life'. Sadly, this definition makes little reference to sustainability. It is a definition which raises a deeply complex issue, yet appears to close down scope for further debate as the term itself becomes a convenient label, used to justify a given course of action. In much the same way as we accept restrictions on our behaviour, the knee-jerk obligation to remove our shoes before boarding an aeroplane for example, without arguing the case, 'food security' becomes a dangerous mantra, under which the possibilities for exploring other options can be diminished.

As I said, even 'food security', or 'insecurity' to give it an alternative perspective, comes packed with its own ideological battlefield. In times of scarcity, the term food security implies a need to address the problem of volume, an inherent need to increase the amount of food we produce. Whilst that may indeed be the case, and the fact that large numbers of people both globally and in Britain, continue to go hungry on a daily basis, the term might be used to reinforce the call for such an increase, and the issue of distribution is easily overlooked. The ideological divide within the notion of food security can be described through the following two perspectives: On the one hand, there is a belief that the primary cause of hunger and food insecurity is rooted in poverty and lack of socioeconomic access to food (in other words, distribution), rather than insufficient food production or overpopulation. It is possible to see this perspective dating back over the centuries, and it might chime with the sentiments of some of the food rioters so far described in this book. On the other hand, and in a perspective which clearly follows on from the sentiments advanced throughout the Green Revolution, food insecurity is best tackled through scientific development geared towards increasing production and the volume of food available. That development also clearly includes the use of genetic modification and brings with it a food fight which appears almost impossible to settle.

One of the problems of GM is its capacity to distract. Those engaged in the emotive argument, debating the perceived rights and wrongs of interfering with nature at a genetic level, together with any concerns over effects that GM may or may not have in the future, often overlook a key element of the practise of genetic modification. Those ensconced in such a debate run the risk of missing a more pressing point. Surely the question of ownership of intellectual property rights over GM seed ought to generate more concern than a seemingly unfathomable ideological debate? It is perhaps within this area of 'food security' that there is scope for a decent food fight, and one which is already beginning to stir. Those corporations which benefit financially through GM appear to be at an advantage. By maintaining a focus solely on quantity of food, and a perceived need to increase that quantity, then the argument appears stacked in favour of those who espouse the merits of genetically modified crops, which can offer protection against disease, as well as increased yields. In a hungry world, however, the capacity for companies such as Monsanto to control food production is backed up by intellectual property rights law. Peter Melchett, policy director of the Soil Association, has pointed out that GM is a top down approach, driven not by the needs of farmers, consumers or the environment, but by those of seed and chemical companies.[4] With genetic modification comes a battle for the ownership of patents, together with laws designed to protect such intellectual property. Award winning broadcaster, writer on sustainable food systems and trustee of the Food Ethics Council, Geoff Tansey, suggests that a more accurate reflection of reality would be to ditch the term 'intellectual property rights' in this case, and talk of 'business monopoly (or exclusionary) privileges',[5] instead. Tansey's observation helps illustrate a concern with genetic modification and the quest for food security, which goes beyond the 'messing with nature/is it safe?' argument and is actually far more relevant in terms of tackling food poverty in the twenty-first century. Tansey goes on to say that:

> In the 21st century, new institutions producing global rules are reshaping the framework in which people concerned with food operate – from smallholders and farm families to global corporations. However, because of the political weight which they command in developed countries, the latter have a disproportionate impact in shaping the increasingly changing global rules within which different actors in the food system have to operate.[6]

I met with Geoff at his home in a West Yorkshire market town. He is clearly sceptical of a system in which the prevailing economic model (namely the free market) is left alone to determine the amount of food which reaches the hungry. Geoff is keen to challenge the notion of a free market, 'all markets have rules', he says, 'it's a question of what those rules are and whose interests they serve best'. I have to say that I share that scepticism. It is true to say that while people on both sides of the argument are frequently engaged in a debate over the morality of genetic engineering, which may or may not prove disastrous for the human race at some point in the future, the more immediate notion of ownership and control of food markets is lost in the argument. The institutions which are reshaping the frameworks, which Tansey mentions, include (though by no means exclusively) corporations like Monsanto, Unilever and DuPont. Through their rigorous pursuit of and protection of intellectual property rights, these corporations are also reshaping the framework of the global food chain. More than that, they are manoeuvring themselves into a position from which they are able to control the global food chain. As we discussed this point over a cup of tea in his study, Tansey raised a point, which struck home; 'the advancement of intellectual property rights over seed production is equivalent to the expansion of the enclosures of the eighteenth century'. It restricts a person's access to a once common resource. And from this perspective, it appears once again, that enclosure is being used in order to facilitate the development of modern farming methods.

Governments, either wittingly or otherwise, are signing up to agreements such as the G8 New Alliance for Food Security and Nutrition, which wrest control from individuals, and redirect it into the hands of the giant corporations. Established in 2012, the New Alliance for Food Security and Nutrition (see those reassuring words 'food security' in there again), is a global initiative ostensibly convened for the greater good. It was introduced as a new phase of global investment in food security, and cited as bringing the capacity to lift millions from food poverty. Its critics hold that the new legislation serves to benefit investors and will operate to the detriment of small farmers and individuals as millions of hectares of land are made available through long-term leases to foreign investors in African, and other 'third world' countries. Tansey holds that this, and a growing mix of global rules affecting food and agriculture has made life more complicated for governments, researchers, industry and civil society groups.[7] I would say that that is putting it mildly. Even more recently, the global market, or more specifically the companies which make up the global market, have pushed for a trade deal which has further opened the rift between business interests and trade unions and civil rights campaigners. The Transatlantic Trade and Investment Partnership (TTIP), which covers the broad gamut of industries and not just those concerned with the production of food, looks set to usher in an era in which private companies are able to wield control over the governments in the countries in which they invest. Critics of TTIP hold that under the Investor State Dispute Settlement clause of the agreement, large companies will be able to sue governments where domestic legislation may affect the profit levels of those companies. Whilst clearly a detailed account of TTIP is without the scope of this book, agreements such as this, together with the New Alliance for Food Security and Nutrition, for example, serve to highlight the capacity of the free market to interfere with the rights of the individual by undermining the democratic process.

Take, for example, the global commercial seed market. It's as if seeds have become bullets in the fight for food, you can only fire them once, and those who produce them stand to benefit most. It is perhaps of little surprise that the top three corporations, Monsanto, Syngenta and DuPont also happen to be leaders in the pesticide market too. In for a penny, in for a pound, I'd say. According to a report published in 2013, by Eco Nexus and Berne Declaration, farmers are compelled each year to buy new seed due to an increase in the use of hybrid seeds, which fail to reproduce reliably and are not worth saving for the next sowing season. In addition, intellectual property rights on seeds prohibit the saving of seeds and seed exchange between farmers.[8] George Monbiot wrote too, in 2013, of practises employed in Mozambique, where the government there is obliged to 'systematically cease distribution of free and unimproved seeds', while drawing up new laws granting intellectual property rights in seeds which will 'promote private sector investment'.[9] To say that things are becoming a little complicated is something of an understatement, but clearly protecting intellectual property rights is about protecting profit, and protecting profit affects the price of food. It is largely the price of food which has lead, not just to the historical riots we have so far encountered within these pages, but also to others which have erupted beyond these shores in more recent times.

There is a widespread school of thought that holds that the whole of the recent 'Arab Spring' and the ensuing political disruption across the Middle East, emerged from what were basically food riots. The Arab Spring is seen by some as a response to concerns over food security. Despots, dictators and long-standing presidents throughout the region have all been affected by the so called 'Arab Spring'. In each of the countries affected, governments have always attempted to ensure that their people could afford the most basic of food in the form of bread. Over the years I've had the pleasure and good fortune to visit many of the countries which have witnessed political and social upheaval in these recent times of crisis. In my travels through Morocco, Tunisia, Egypt, Jordan and Syria I often saw queues outside nondescript buildings, government funded bakeries, where citizens could buy subsidized bread on a daily basis. The simple link between political stability and the availability of basic food was there to be seen, politics of provision exemplified. In each of the countries I visited, the respective governments had maintained a grip on a closed economy and in doing so were able to affect the price of food. Clearly it was not just the price of a loaf of bread that maintained the longevity of many dictatorial regimes, secret police forces, appalling human rights records and a not inconsiderable degree of terror also played a significant part, but the link remains none the less. In a region which remains heavily dependent on imported food, each of the countries are highly susceptible to price hikes. The spike in food prices which occurred between 2007 and 2008 had a truly dramatic effect. In his book, *Endless Appetite: how the commodities casino creates hunger and unrest*, journalist Alan Bjerga describes what has perhaps become one of the most tragic and iconic events of recent years. In December 2010, on a street in the city of Sidi Bouzid in central Tunisia, Mohamed Bouazizi, a vendor of fruit and vegetables, set fire to himself in protest at his treatment by the local authorities who set out to confiscate his wares. Struggling to earn a living and support his family in the face of rising food prices, Bouazizi took his concerns to the local government office. When officials refused to listen, the street vendor doused himself in paint thinners and struck a match. Less than three weeks later, Mohamed Bouazizi died of his wounds. The Tunisian government was overthrown just ten days later.[10] Such was the support for Bouazizi, and the rage which he expressed in the most tragic of ways, the people of Tunisia took to the streets and ousted a President who had held on to power for almost a quarter of a century. Riots quickly spread across North Africa, through Algeria, Libya and Egypt, to other parts of the Middle East. I contacted Syrian journalist Ibrahim Hamidi, now based in London and head of the Syria desk at *Al Hayat* newspaper. Ibrahim offered further insight into the link between the uprisings in the region and the rising prices of food. Again, the notion of an uprising, which stems from a lack of food comes to the fore, although Ibrahim was at pains to suggest that in the case of the Syrian uprising, which began in 2011, there were clearly a number of factors at play. Ibrahim steered me in the direction of a study published in January 2014 in the journal *Middle Eastern Studies*, in which the author suggests that alongside a degree of climate change enhanced draught, a fair degree of resource mismanagement and over exploitation led to disenfranchizement and discontent in Syria's rural communities.[11]

Apparently it was more than a mere hunger for democracy which drove hundreds of thousands of protestors onto the streets and led to the overthrow of several governments. It may just have been plain old hunger itself. As far back as 2008 the clues were there. CNN and other western media sources reported the spread of rioting and instability as food prices skyrocketed. In 2011 a detailed study was submitted at the New England Complex Systems Institute in the United States, which looked at 'The Food Crises and Political Instability in North Africa and the Middle East'. The study was picked up and reported by the *Guardian* newspaper (which at the time also stated that the report had yet to undergo peer review). The paper has since been widely cited as it identifies a specific food price threshold, above which protests become likely, and suggests that protests may be a result of the long-standing failings of governments, as well as the sudden desperate financial conditions of vulnerable populations. The research refers to historical 'food riots' across Europe following the drought of 1848, and recognizes their consequent challenges to authority and political change. The authors go on to note that today's high dependency, on behalf of 'poor countries', upon the global food supply system lays them open to vulnerability, particularly in the face of increasing food price fluctuation. In a separate paper, the authors attribute recent food price hikes to a significant rise in crops grown solely for biofuel production, as well as investor speculation on commodity markets. Perhaps more alarmingly the Food Crises and political instability report also acknowledges broader repercussions of such dependency and issue a caution, not just to policy makers in undeveloped countries but the rest of the world, also, as desperate populations are likely to resort to violence even in democratic regimes:

> This understanding suggests that reconsidering biofuel policy as well as commodity market regulations should be an urgent priority for policymakers. Reducing the amount of corn converted to ethanol, and restricting commodity future markets to bona fide risk hedging would reduce global food prices. The current problem transcends the specific national political crises to represent a global concern about vulnerable populations and social order.[12]

It will be interesting to see the extent (if any) to which this warning is heeded by governments across the world, and the way in which any remedial action is set out. I'm not holding out much hope. From an historical perspective in the UK, it is possible to see the extent to which governments dealt decisively with food rioters and those protesting for their right to feed their families, both through legislation as well as prosecution, particularly during the nineteenth century, at a time when the governments concerned felt threatened by the prospect of revolution. In the twenty-first century, and in Britain at least, the very existence of 'food poverty' is now hotly debated. A report commissioned by the Department for Environment, Food and Rural Affairs (DEFRA) was released in February 2014. Publication of the report was originally expected in the summer of 2013, and was anticipated as providing the foundation for improving government, business and civil society's understanding of food aid provision in Britain. Delays in publication brought urgent calls from opposition members in the House of Commons. Frank Field, Labour MP for the Wirral, tabled a Commons motion with the support of 72 MPs and the report was finally released after a significant period of 'review and quality control' by DEFRA.

To say that the DEFRA report lacked punch would be an understatement. In a manner which appears not entirely removed from the flippancy of Marie Antoinette's famous remark regarding the eating of cake, the main conclusion in the document appeals to a need for more research. Furthermore, the authors of the report, which was carried out by staff at the University of Warwick, take time at the head of the report to stress that the research was not asked specifically to address the impact of public policies on social security. It's clear to me that the authors of the report may have felt that there was scope for a much more detailed investigation. Whilst claiming it impossible to give an accurate estimate of the numbers of people fed by food aid, a key finding of the research states that turning to food aid is a strategy of last resort, when households have exhausted all other strategies, these include cutting back and changing eating and shopping habits, juggling budgets and turning to family and friends. In what was presumably a costly exercise, DEFRA managed to commission and then delay publication of a report which states the bleeding obvious. In Britain, as in other countries, the impact of rising food prices has been exacerbated by swathing cuts in the welfare state.

Perhaps in anticipation of the toothless DEFRA report, Labour MP Frank Field, together with Laura Sandys MP, Conservative MP for South Thanet, established an All Party Parliamentary Group (APPG) on Hunger and Food Poverty in the UK in October 2013. In February of 2014, the APPG announced it was to commission a Parliamentary Inquiry into food poverty in Britain. The group published the preliminary findings of its nascent investigation in June 2014 after hearing evidence presented from around the country. Having received evidence that the rising cost of housing, food and fuel has had an adverse impact on households' ability to buy and cook meals, an early recommendation of the group is that the food industry should set itself a target of reducing the amount of surplus food disposed of in landfill (instead turning it into compost or energy) by 1,000,000 tonnes each year.

Commenting on the preliminary recommendations, Frank Field MP and Bishop of Truro Tim Thornton, acknowledge that:

> The poorest households have most felt the pinch over the past decade, meaning the last resort of turning to food banks has become a reality for an increasing number of people. There is a real need for help. We are setting out some immediate steps we feel could stop people from going hungry now, by making better use of the food we do have. We're calling for a real focus on the millions of tonnes of surplus food that goes to waste each year in the food retail sector. Our proposals would save charities money, put downward pressure on food prices and provide healthier options to families relying on voluntary support.[13]

The final report, 'Feeding Britain', was published in December 2014. It concluded that hunger in Britain is here to stay until counteraction is taken. The report also went on to say that appropriate action is not only desirable, but possible. A total of 77 recommendations were put forward by the authors of the report as it examined a number of areas, which were either seen to contribute to a growth in food poverty, or were areas in which hunger and food poverty were abundantly clear. They included Hunger in Schools, Low Pay, Debt and High Cost Credit, Benefit Administration, Resilience – cooking, parenting and budgeting. The first recommendation was the formation of a national network called 'Feeding Britain', to be composed of the food bank movement and other food charities, the food industry, and representatives from each of the eight government departments whose policy affects the number of people at risk of hunger. A coordinated body through which to direct and tackle efforts at reducing food poverty.

The 'Feeding Britain' report detailed accounts of food banks which were consistently under-supplied, as well as lacking the facility or resources to supply fresh and perishable food to their clients. In its evidence gathering, the APPG heard from a host of charities and projects which engaged in tackling food poverty and helping to distribute 'waste food' to the less well off. Such projects will be examined in more detail in a later chapter. Whilst clearly a concise, detailed and meticulous examination of food poverty and hunger is a welcome step forward, what is alarming and perhaps (for the more cynical among us) ominous is the disclaimer at the head of the report, which states that the publication is not an official publication, nor has it been approved by parliament or any of its committees.

In what might begin to resemble a plethora of recent reports and investigations into food poverty, the Fabian Society also hosted a year long investigation into the subject. Chaired by Geoff Tansey, and with a panel of experts drawn from a number of disciplines including food policy, health, social policy, education and the environment, the investigation heard evidence from across the country. The commission travelled to several different regions to hear stories and gather research from a range of individuals and organizations. The interim report 'A Recipe for Inequality' was published in March 2015, and seems to have gone some way towards digging deeper than other investigations, and talks in terms of the price of food system failure. The final report, 'Hungry for Change', was published in October 2015.

Taking a different approach to the APPG, and with a focus on the relationship between food and poverty, rather than looking directly at food charity itself, the Fabian Commission on Food and Poverty was keen to investigate how a fairer food system can be built that works better for people on low incomes. At the head of the report, the commission uncovers what it refers to as a 'crisis of food access for many households in the UK'. It goes on to describe this condition as 'household food insecurity': the inability to acquire or consume an adequate quality or sufficient quantity of food in socially acceptable ways. 'Hungry for Change' suggests a total of thirteen action points which would aid progress towards ending household food insecurity. Like the 'Feeding Britain' report, the Fabian Commission on Food and Poverty suggest that the government should take a greater responsibility for combating food poverty across the board.

Whilst it is clear to see that the nature of the food fight has changed, with new areas of conflict opening up as technology is increasingly applied to the food chain, what hasn't changed is the impact of the affordability and availability of food upon the poor. That problem just won't seem to go away. The fact that the amorphous mass of 'the poor' is growing exponentially, in a modern Britain wrapped in a horsehair blanket of austerity, is one which would suggest that there is still a role for the food rioter to play. Our eating habits have changed over the years, so too has the way we shop for food. The industrialization of the food chain, which began on an unprecedented scale after the Second World War, paved the way for what seemed to be a natural progression; the rise of the supermarket.

END NOTES

1. Monbiot, G. *Captive State*, p.225.
2. Oliver Wright in *The Independent*, 13 October 2013.
3. Carson, R. *Silent Spring*, p. 174.
4. EFRA report 'Food Security', July 2014.
5. Tansey, G. *The Future of Food Control*, p.17.
6. Ibid. p.6.
7. Ibid. p.171.
8. *Eco Nexus Report* 2013 - Agropoly; a handful of corporations control world food.
9. George Monbiot, in the *Guardian*, 11 June 2013.
10. Bjerga, A. *Endless Appetites*, p.4.
11. De Chatel, F. 'The Role of Drought and Climate Change in the Syrian Uprising: Untangling the Triggers of the Revolution', in *Middle Eastern Studies*, L/iv, 2014.
12. Lagi, Bertram & Bar Yam - *Food Crises and political instability*, (2011), p.6
13. http://foodpovertyinquiry.org

CHAPTER EIGHT

THE RISE OF THE SUPERMARKETS

The origins of the supermarket are steeped in social purpose. They emerged initially as co-operative societies formed among the working classes as a means of securing a supply of good quality food for their members. With obvious connections to, and sharing similarities with the 'seditious' benefit clubs of the eighteenth century, the first co-operatives date from the 1760s. The objectives of the early pioneers were to buy up food wholesale and to sell at retail prices and to divide any dividend among members on an annual basis. In effect, the aim was to cut out the middle man. By the middle of the nineteenth century, the number of co-operative societies had grown and members were able to buy tea, sugar, flour and other groceries under one roof. By 1914, the numbers of co-operative society members was in excess of 3 million, and the overall business had a turnover of £100 million.[1] Despite the rise of the co-operative society, throughout the 1950s and 1960s, people also continued to shop locally, calling at greengrocers, fishmongers and butchers shops for their weekly supply of food.

Retailers like J. Sainsbury, Tesco and William Morrison realized the commercial potential of the co-operative model, and in particular, the 'one stop shop'. They were keen to get in on the act. They began to expand during the 1960s, floating their companies on the stock exchange, attracting shareholders rather than members. The era of self-service supermarket shopping was born. Rapid expansion during the 1970s and 1980s saw a sea change in the way modern families bought their food. Technology too, fed this expansion. The widespread availability of domestic freezers, which grew during the late 1960s and early 1970s, also marked a change in the types of food that modern families were buying, as well as the way they were cooking and eating. The new supermarkets were able to stock large quantities of frozen food, and an ever increasing range of 'ready meals' which apparently suited the lifestyles of busy home cooks. Supermarkets brought with them the apparent benefit of saving time on the weekly shop, but perhaps more importantly, through their bulk buying power and its corresponding influence over the food chain, supermarkets were able to further drive the retail price down to suit the pockets of their customers. It is a marketing technique that clearly worked. It is also a marketing technique which brings with it a number of dire consequences. According to the Office of National Statistics (ONS), food stores account for over 40% of total retail sales in the UK. The vast majority of spending takes place in what the ONS calls 'non-specialised food stores', namely supermarkets. The top five retailers have around 75% of market share in a groceries market worth a total of £146 billion.[2] The ONS also describes an average weekly spend for a family of two adults with two children, of £82.90. It is fair to say that the majority of our food is bought from supermarkets. This trend towards cheap is bolstered with the recent arrival of 'price busting' competitors Lidl and Aldi challenging the domination of the top flight supermarket stores. The broader impact of these new interlocutors has yet to be recognized, but it appears that supermarket bosses are committed to delivering low cost food to the market.

There is a school of thought, and Professor Tim Lang at City University London is arguably the head teacher of that school, that points out that the government's adoption of a 'cheap food policy' dates back to the mid nineteenth century with the abolition of the Corn Laws. The repeal of the Corn Laws in 1846, a demand made by the emerging industrialists who wanted cheaper imported food for their low wage workforce,[3] paved the way for the market alone to determine prices once more. The riot act of 1715 and the often brutal methods of dealing with public disturbance around food markets had all but removed the public from any negotiation. More recently, since the early 1970s, Britain has enjoyed access to cheap food and that access has been facilitated by the rapid expansion of supermarket shopping. Consumers as well as producers, however, have inadvertently become collateral damage in a never ending price war, a drive for higher profits and customer loyalty. Supermarkets continue to do battle in a bid to maintain the flow of customers through their doors, perpetuating a highly flawed market model that results in mountains of food waste that is detrimental to both producers, and ultimately the consumers themselves. Over production is the corner stone of the supermarket business model. It means that supermarket buyers are able to wield control over the prices they pay to producers, as well as slash their orders at a moments notice. All the while there is an abundance of produce out there, growers are more or less forced to dance to the tune of the supermarket jingle. I've worked in a supermarket and I know how annoying that can be. Through bombarding customers with two -for-one offers, offering cheaper prices and seemingly endless choice, the predominant paradigm has led to a reduction in the production of domestically produced food in this country. It is now often cheaper to import food from abroad, while farmers and producers find it increasingly difficult to make ends meet. Jay Rayner, in his book *A Greedy Man in a Hungry World* examines the 'supermarkets are evil/supermarkets are not evil' paradox. It is of note that Mr Rayner dedicates a mere fourteen pages to the claim that supermarkets are not evil, and an additional ten pages to the chapter which suggests the opposite. Rayner illustrates well the effect of supermarkets' buying power on the welfare of British farmers, citing the case of a plum grower whose entire crop was left to fall from the branches and rot as the supermarkets bought in cheaper plums from abroad. The role of the consumer too must be taken into consideration in this price war. It is difficult to determine whether it is solely consumer demand or supermarkets' capacity for squeezing margins (at the expense of producers and their own staff) which feeds the perpetual drive for cheap food. Common sense would seem to indicate that it's a bit of both, but not necessarily in equal portions.

Supermarkets seem to hit the headlines on a regular basis these days, often under a cloud. In 2014, Tesco ran into trouble on account of its over aggressive accounting practises as it was found to have over estimated its profits to the tune of £250 million. If the market squares of towns and villages were the scene of food riots in previous centuries, it is almost impossible to envisage such events taking place today. Beyond the odd scuffle in the reduced items section, it is difficult to imagine scenes of tumult and affray in a market place defined by aisles and fridges packed with special offers and falling prices. There are of course exceptions here and there. More recently, the falling price of milk has brought farmer and retailer to loggerheads. In August 2015, in a fitting protest by dairy farmers, and highly symbolic of the store's origins, staff and customers at ASDA were surprised to witness a couple of cows being herded around the store in Stafford. Somewhat ironically, ASDA was born in the 1960s of a merger between a family of butchers and a group of dairy farmers originally seeking to protect themselves from falling prices of milk. The protest was part of a series of nationwide actions taken by farmers to highlight the fact that some supermarkets refuse to guarantee a price for milk which covers its production. The protests appear to have had an effect as a number of supermarkets agreed to offer a higher price to the their milk suppliers.

But to a degree, the evil/not evil question is an arbitrary point, and to get into a debate as to whether supermarkets are good things or bad things is similar in its nature to the debate over the 'morality' of genetically modified crops, a case of 'divide and rule' if you like. It merely serves to divert attention from more pressing matters. Namely the devastating effect that some supermarkets can have on individual farmers and producers, not to mention the control they have over the food system as a whole. Somewhat ironically, supermarkets contribute daily to a growing mountain of food waste. The model of pile 'em high and sell 'em cheap is clearly not working as despite, or perhaps because of, all efforts to offer food at lowest prices to their customers, supermarkets are increasingly coming under the scrutiny of governments worldwide, with regard to the amount of food they throw out each day. Food waste is one of the points that the parliamentary inquiry in 2014 and the 'Hungry for Change' reports appears to have picked up on and is currently the focus of much attention. To my mind, the 15 million tonnes of food waste generated annually in Britain[4] alone goes some considerable way to belittling the argument from the GM lobby of a need to increase crop yields. With fields and orchards full of perfectly good food left to rot it would appear that a case could be made to the effect that there is enough food to go round, and that it is access to that food which ought best be examined by government. I doubt very much that the waste generating food system we have at the moment will ever be used as a counter to the GM lobby, but it is increasingly attracting the attention of the British public. What I find interesting is the way in which supermarkets (and arguably the government), although perhaps slow to start off with, have suddenly realized that spread of food poverty in Britain presents a relatively low cost solution to the issue of what to do with the growing mountains of food waste. The only problem is that it is neither a solution in its own right, nor is it sustainable.

In 2013, the UK government set up a 'watchdog', the Groceries Code Adjudicator (GCA), in a bid to ensure that supermarkets treat their suppliers fairly and lawfully. Within a very short space of time, the GCA came under fire from the farmers it was set up to protect and is castigated as a watch dog without teeth as the powers of the adjudicator appear limited vis-à-vis the might of the supermarkets. It's a dispute which could be seen to echo that of the landed gentry and gentlemen farmers versus the industrialists back in the mid nineteenth century over the repeal of the Corn Laws. Once again, the industrialists (supermarkets in this case) appear to come out on top.

The financial pressures on supermarket bosses, and the need to satisfy shareholders rather than members has a marked effect on their practises. In order to ensure low prices for customers, clearly overheads such as wage bills are also kept to a minimum. It's not just supermarket employees however that appear to suffer as a consequence, but customers too. In 2013, a number of supermarkets ran into trouble as a lack of integrity in their supply chains was revealed amid the horsemeat scandal. Attempting to pass off cheaper horsemeat as beef is akin to adulteration and marks a return to the days of a handful of gravel in the sack of corn. We witness the compromise of price over quality. Unlike the co-operatives which preceded them, supermarkets' primary motives are geared around profits. That is not necessarily a bad thing in itself, but what is needed is an understanding of the broader effects such a model has on the food chain as a whole. To what extent, if any, does the dominance of supermarkets in our food system contribute to growth of food poverty in Britain? In the following chapter, we discover that a number of supermarkets are keen to establish their community credentials and contribute willingly to food banks and food recycling schemes with donations of waste food from their distribution centres, food that never even makes it onto the supermarket shelves.

END NOTES

1. Burnett, J. *Plenty and Want*, p.146.
2. GCA fact file: https://www.gov.uk/government/uploads/system/uploads/attachment_data/file/226119/GCA_Supporting_facts_and_QAs_July_2013.pdf
3. Professor Tim Lang: http://theconversation.com/how-to-end-britains-destructive-addiction-to-food-banks-50096
4. 'Hungry For Change' report, 2015 p.18.

CHAPTER NINE

FOOD POVERTY AND FOOD CHARITY IN BRITAIN TODAY

During the Middle Ages, and up until the early sixteenth century, poor relief was largely in the hands of the church. Those living in poverty often relied on the monasteries to provide food, and in some cases employment. With the dissolution of the monasteries between 1530 and 1541, much of the responsibility for poor relief began to pass over to the state, as the monasteries faced a dismal future. Almost five centuries later, it is possible to see that a cycle of repetition is in train. As the 'shocking' rise of food bank use in Britain is proclaimed in newspaper headlines on an almost daily basis, it is clear to see that a significant proportion of those organizations administering food parcels to hungry citizens, are faith-based organizations. Poor relief, it seems, is back in the hands of the church.

In May 2013, the Church Action on Poverty group, together with Oxfam, published a report, 'Walking the Breadline - the scandal of food poverty in 21ˢᵗ century Britain'. This report appeared to kick up a bit of a storm. It estimated that over 500,000 people are reliant on food aid in this country. Citing an earlier report commissioned and carried out by famed cereal producers Kellogg's, it claimed that four out of five teachers reported that some of their children were arriving at school hungry,[1] and that it was affecting their capacity to learn. 'Walking the Breadline' went a long way towards raising the profile of food poverty in Britain and made clear assertions of the link between welfare benefit reform and food poverty. It arguably lead to the commissioning of the DEFRA report, which was consequently buried and finally released in February 2014.

In February 2014, religious leaders in Britain spoke out against welfare reforms and accused the government of creating a climate of 'hardship and hunger'. In a letter to the Prime Minister, signed by 27 Anglican Bishops and 16 other clergy, the religious leaders pointed out the explosion in the use of food banks in Britain, as well as the number of people admitted to hospital for malnutrition.[2] The letter marked the inauguration of the 'End Hunger Fast' campaign. Stating clearly the campaign's belief that no one should go hungry in Britain, while recognizing that more and more people are just one unexpected bill away from facing bare cupboards, End Hunger Fast highlighted what it referred to as a 'national and moral crisis' and called upon the government to protect the hundreds of thousands of people going hungry in Britain in 2014. The campaign was intentionally short-lived, but its work continues to tackle hunger through the actions of its partner organizations, including the Trussell Trust and the Church Action on Poverty Group.

I met with Ben Haldene, Manager at Bradford Central Food Bank, in March 2014. Bradford Central Food Bank lies in the shadow of the city's cathedral, and save for a small plaque on the wall outside the door you wouldn't know it was there. Food banks are a little reluctant to advertize their presence, and this sits well with their clients, as many are often 'embarrassed' at having to resort to such charity. In an interview which lasted the best part of two hours, I felt as though I was being transported back to the nineteenth century and beyond. Bradford Central Food Bank is run on the 'social franchise' model put forward by The Trussell Trust, and apart from full-time manager Ben, relies on volunteers to run the operation. The Trussell Trust was first established, with its roots planted firmly in Christian tradition, in a garden shed in Salisbury, Wiltshire, back in 2000. Set-up by Paddy and Carol Henderson, who had worked for a UN feeding programme in Bulgaria, the organization has since grown and now operates over 400 food banks across the country through its 'social franchise' system. Working closely with existing communities in towns and cities throughout the UK, Trussell Trust food banks have witnessed an exponential rise in the numbers of people being offered a three-day emergency food parcel. The numbers of people receiving 'food aid' from Trust food banks has witnessed an almost threefold increase from 350,000 in 2012/13, to over 900,000 in 2013/14.[3] Time spent with Ben Haldene painted an even more harrowing perspective on these statistics. Among the 4,875 people given assistance by Ben's team, between 1st March 2013 and the end of February 2014, a significant number of recipients were given food parcels specifically designed for people who could not afford to cook the food being donated. I was staggered to find that, and this is not uncommon across many food banks as many recipients of food aid have only the use of a kettle with which to heat their food. Such is the poverty among some in modern Britain, and in a scenario which shares a characteristic from the enclosure acts back in the nineteenth century, some people can no longer afford the fuel necessary to cook their food.

The very use of 'kettle boxes', food parcels containing basics such as instant mashed potato, noodles and instant soup, appears to illustrate the varying degrees of poverty faced by families left with little option but to queue at food banks. It also raises concerns for the nutritional content of the so called 'kettle boxes'. I was dumbfounded. When I asked Ben what brought his 'guests' to his doors – I was intrigued by his use of the word guest, as opposed to 'client' or 'service user', it brings with it a much more personal feel to the whole affair and keeps the whole show grounded in humanity – what reasons they were citing for their attendance at the food bank, he replied with a ready list of 'causes' which practically rolled off the tip of his tongue:

benefit delays, change and sanction, low incomes, debt, domestic violence and delayed wages. The evidence flies in the face of repeated government edicts denying any link between a reduction in state benefits and food poverty. It's a denial that adds an interesting angle to this investigation of 'food fights', and one which alters the dynamic of the food fight to an apparent battle now pitched between the government and the voluntary sector, rather than one of communities versus farmers which was common to some food fights gone by. In some respects, it mimics the battle between Frankenstein and the monster, the so called 'Big Society', it seems, has emerged to do battle with the prime minister who 'created it'. A prevailing echo from the DEFRA Report which was released in February 2014, following a long period of 'tinkering' by the government before it was eventually released, was that there is a paucity of information regarding the extent of 'food aid' networks in the UK. The report states:

> Beyond public information from national charities [such as The Trussell Trust Foodbank Network] there is little evidence of a 'food aid system' as such within the UK, as has emerged in some other countries with a longer history of charitable or state provision. Independent local initiatives in the UK are currently hard to capture in data monitoring or research.[4]

Where else, one might ask, would a researcher look for evidence of a 'food aid' system, beyond those national charities which are clearly engaged on a daily basis in distributing food parcels to the poor. This prevarication on behalf of the government, over acknowledging the recent explosion in food aid and charity provision, feels to me like a resurgence of the arrogance displayed by the ruling classes towards the poor of the eighteenth century, 'let them eat three minute noodles'. As for the alleged difficulties of capturing data from local independent initiatives, the APPG *Feeding Britain* report actively sought evidence from a number of food charities, and welcomed their expertize. I certainly found no difficulty in Bradford. Ben certainly had more than a little information about the operations of the project. A reasonable amount of time in Ben's working day is given over to recording, in meticulous detail, statistics relating to the work carried out by the food bank; ethnicity, family make-up, age groups of service users, as well as reasons for referral are all recorded on a ward-by-ward basis. The evidence is there; Benefit Delays, Benefit Changes, Low Income, Debt, Domestic Violence, delayed and low wages, are all there as reasons cited by Ben's 'guests' for using the food bank. Evidence collected by this food bank alone, shows that food poverty is not solely restricted to deprived 'inner city' areas, with referrals coming in from every ward (more than thirty including subdivisions of larger wards) under Bradford Metropolitan District Council's jurisdiction.

That the government should initially go to such lengths to 'suppress' its own investigation into food poverty (as outlined in the closing paragraphs of chapter seven), both by limiting the scope of the investigation as well as delaying its publication almost beggars belief. It's a far cry from the grounded admissions of previous libertarian governments during the eighteenth and nineteenth centuries, which indicated that poverty (and resulting food riots) were an 'accepted pressure valve' through which the inequalities of society might be vented. The *Guardian* newspaper columnist, Owen Jones echoed this in his 2011 book *'Chavs' - the demonization of the working class*:

> Social problems like poverty and unemployment were once understood as injustices that sprang from flaws within capitalism which, at the very least, had to be addressed. Yet today they have become understood as the consequences of personal behaviour, individual defects and even choice.[5]

In the twenty-first century, the very notion of a connection twixt poverty and hunger seems moot, at least according to the government. More to the point, we appear to be witnessing a rise in notions of 'the undeserving poor' as lifestyle choice and individual behaviour are put forward as reasons for poverty at the expense, or denial, of any other possible contributing factors. Using terminology which harks back to descriptions of the 'undeserving poor' dwelling in 'riotous squalor' in their hovels on the common, attacks on food banks in right wing newspapers are frequent. In March 2014, the *Daily Mail* was quick to point out that the 10,000[th] visitor to a food bank in Coventry was in fact a 'conman', a ne'er-do-well, with a string of criminal convictions and a propensity for working while claiming benefits.[6] It was cited under the headline, 'The unpalatable truth about food banks, the left finds so hard to swallow'. The 'undeserving poor' are somewhat ironically portrayed as looking for a free lunch, which of course is exactly what they are doing, because they can't afford to buy one. It's as though by castigating the odd rule bender, those opposed (or perhaps embarrassed) by the proliferation of food banks are hoping to destroy any evidence of their need. Millionaire former investment banker, and now (at the time of writing) minister responsible for welfare reform, Lord Freud chose to quote Aaron Antonovski, an Israeli sociologist, at a conference on welfare reform in London in January 2014. He said that:

> If people know why things happen to them, and they have the support and ability to manage their lives, they have a fighting chance of being able to maintain their well-being.

It's an interesting use of words, particularly from one who has repeatedly claimed that 'its hard to know why people go to food banks'. It's clear that the form of 'support', which Freud mentions in this case comes not from the state, but from the broader community, and in particular, the voluntary sector and the church. Food aid, it seems, is beyond the remit of government.

Other attacks on the culture of food banks lay claim to their capacity to feed the black market, as recipients of food parcels may seek to sell their food for cash, either within their local community, or perhaps to unscrupulous shopkeepers seeking to re-sell the goods at a profit. This is clearly a practise to which the Trussell Trust is wise, as Ben Haldene told me the organization was keen to receive and distribute, supermarkets' 'own brand' bread and other goods, as this severely restricted any possibilities for their 'guests' to sell-on the food to convenience store owners. I asked Ben about this, but he was unable to provide any information as to the numbers of food parcel recipients suspected of selling-on items from their parcel. It's clearly a difficult area to monitor and doing so would require detective skills way beyond the remit of food bank volunteers. Even if there are the odd one or two (maybe one or two thousand, who knows?) who choose to exploit this system of food relief, surely that cannot be used as a reason to dismiss the need for food banks altogether. There are other criticisms levelled at food banks, however, which come from the food charity sector itself. Dr Bryce Evans, Senior lecturer in History at Liverpool Hope University, runs what he refers to as a sustainable alternative to food banks, a 'community kitchen' in his spare time. He is not alone in his criticism, some of which is shared by people working for a number of the food charities discussed below. Food banks are seen by some to represent an abrogation of the state's responsibility to its citizens. The reliance on the distribution of non-perishable goods means that their 'guests' are less likely to be able to prepare a nutritionally balanced meal. The model used by many food banks is often described as utterly unsustainable (it is noted in the *Feeding Britain* report that a food bank in Hastings was giving out more food than was donated). The final criticism directed at food banks is that food donations from supermarkets makes the multi million pound industry out to be 'one of the good guys', that is to say supermarkets are easily able to cash-in and polish up their community credentials, even though, as noted in the previous chapter, their domination of the market is a key contributor to the problem in the first place.

The work of the All Party Parliamentary Group has already gone some way to establishing a link between poverty and the rise of food aid provision. Even in its preliminary findings, the group suggested ways of alleviating pressure on low income families by attempting to reduce food prices. By focusing on food waste, and seeking to promote re-distribution of surplus, or waste food from supermarkets and other shops, the APPG Inquiry heard evidence from a number of organizations which, in many ways can be seen to be employing a tactic used by food rioters of the eighteenth century. It's not quite the act of seizing a cart load of corn on its way to market, but the similarities are there to be seen. The redistribution element of such enterprises, in my view, chimes with practises of the Gloucestershire Bread rioters. The main difference today of course, being that the supermarkets (from where much of the 'recycled' food is garnered) have already banked their profits. There is clear evidence in this country of a food aid system, it's just that it has drifted beyond the scope of provision under the welfare state, and local groups and communities appear to be doing it for themselves. The government, it seems, is happy just to let those charities get on with it.

Initiatives and organizations such as 'Fare Share', Community shop and 'Foodcycle', have been making use of 'surplus' food from supermarkets and food producers for a number of years, distributing the food to charities and community projects throughout the country. Similarly, organizations such as Brighton-based Food Waste Collective, and Feedback, the organization behind Gleaning Network UK, are encouraging the re-introduction of the practise of 'Gleaning' – an ancient activity which arguably dates back to biblical times, whereby members of the local community would enter farmland after harvest, to collect or 'glean' any left over produce. Today, volunteers help gather fruit and vegetables that farmers are unable to sell on to supermarkets as they don't meet the aesthetic demands of supermarket buyers, and the produce is then distributed among local charities providing meals for society's less well off. In 2013, Gleaning Network UK gathered over 45,000 tonnes of fresh produce, with new 'gleaning hubs' springing up from Brighton to Manchester.

The reintroduction of gleaning in the UK marks a practise which though effectively outlawed in 1788, continued with the permission of some farmers, and was a feature of English village life right up until the 1950s. By this time, the development of highly efficient new farm machinery had meant that the amounts of crops left over in the fields after harvest had fallen to a point when it no longer made 'economic sense' for the gleaners to continue with their ancient practise. Up until this point it can be said that the opportunity for gleaning fields was presented by the inefficiencies of the harvesting process. The gleaners of today are faced with a bounty which is left behind in the fields, not through inefficient harvesting methods, but one which ought to give much greater cause for alarm, and is perhaps indicative of a food system at fault, particularly in the light of the growing numbers of people in this country who are struggling to feed themselves and their families. Much of the produce which the Gleaning Network gathers today fails the aesthetic test, the quality control of the supermarket buyers. The gleaners of today are picking 'ugly' vegetables, although I would be inclined to suggest that a food system which rejects perfectly edible food purely on aesthetic grounds is ugly in its own right. The modern gleaners of today of course enjoy the active support and encouragement of the farmers who own the land over which they glean. It's a good thing, food that otherwise would go to waste is being put to good use by large numbers of good people. The Gleaning Network is fast growing into a national project, working to coordinate volunteers with farmers up and down the country.

Feedback is a national organization, set up in 2009 by award winning writer and campaigner Tristram Stuart. It runs a number of projects; Feeding the 5000, The Pig Idea and the Gleaning Network, all geared towards utilizing waste food for the benefit of communities. Stuart's book, *Waste: uncovering the global food scandal,* published in the same year by Penguin Books, highlighted the issue of food waste in the global food chain. Both in the book and through setting-up Feedback, Stuart has argued and demonstrated that tackling the problem of food waste is central to relieving pressure on the environment as well as food supplies. Winning the BBC Food and Farming Award for best initiative in British food in 2014, Feedback has brought a vibrancy to the issue of food waste, which appeals to a broad audience and what Fare Share Chief Executive, Lindsay Boswell, calls a culture shift in the attitude to food surpluses and waste. I asked Tristram, in the light of the circumstances surrounding food rioters of previous centuries, to what extent (if any) does he consider the likes of the Gleaning Network as 'food rioters for the twenty-first century'? His answer suggested that such a comparison lacked relevance, and poses a serious challenge to my thesis regarding the continuity of food struggle.

> I think it would be contorted and possibly rather silly to compare the Gleaning Network to literally starving eighteenth century food rioters in such a way. Rioting has a very special place in civilisation: when people are pushed to a point of urgency that society's rules are set aside and violent insurrection is deployed. It's not really appropriate to make the comparison in my view.

He went on to explain that:

> there is a wide range of cultural practices, trends and values that all share in common the view that whilst there is plenty of food available and while food is being wasted, it's not acceptable that people should be going hungry. Exactly how this impacts on individuals and companies morally is open to interpretation. I believe, like Locke, that if food will otherwise be wasted, it's better to make it available for others to eat. I suspect that everyone participating in the Gleaning Network, including the farmers with whose proactive consent we are invited into the fields, is operating on a similar impulse.

To be fair to Tristram, I can see his point, in that in the case of today's gleaners, it's not necessarily the poor and starving that are doing the gleaning, but as I have previously suggested, rather individuals with concerns for the welfare of others perhaps less well off. Another key point here is the proactive consent of the farmers, without which the rebirth of gleaning could not take place. We will return to this point later.

Fare Share began in 1994 as a project run by the homelessness charity Crisis. Ten years later it emerged as an independent charity as the organization grew to provide relief to people in food poverty beyond its original focus on the homeless. A continual cycle of growth has seen the charity open twenty depots and distribution centres across much of the UK, and over 1,200 charities benefit from

Fare Share food, saving them some £16 million.[7] Fare Share does not distribute food to individuals, rather it donates food to local charities and projects dedicated to helping those less well off. By establishing working partnerships with supermarkets such as Sainsbury's, Asda and Tesco, Fare Share has gained access to supply chains and is able to recycle surplus fresh food from supermarket distribution centres. It has developed a business model which keys-in to, and benefits from the huge expense that supermarkets face in disposing of their surplus food. By taking surplus food off the hands of the large retailers, Fare Share effectively saves supermarkets money and provides an ideal framework through which to deliver their own community conscious commitments.

Community Shop opened the doors to the country's first 'social supermarket' in Goldthorpe, Rotherham South Yorkshire in 2013. The store offers discounts on some foods of up to 70% to its members, and enjoys the support of a number of national supermarkets as well as food producers. Members of the Community Shop must be in receipt of specific benefits in order to access discounted food. Sited within 'hotspots of deprivation', Community Shops are a 'members only' way of ensuring that people on low incomes have access to cheap, good quality food. Sharing similarities with the 'benefit clubs' of years past, Community Shops are run by volunteers and also offer other services to their members including CV writing skills, cookery classes and skills training.

Foodcycle emerged from a makeshift pop-up kitchen in 2008, and was the brainchild of Kelvin Cheung who stepped down as Chief Executive Officer in 2013, handing the reins to Mary McGrath. The organization has since grown, with food cycle 'hubs' operating across the country. Working directly with local charities, Foodcycle volunteers use 'recycled' waste food to provide meals, and community cafés for socially excluded people. Operating on a similar model to, and in partnership with Fare Share, Foodcycle embrace the notion of food as a building block of communities. I met with Lydia, the Hub Leader of the Leeds branch of Foodcycle. I joined the meeting as Lydia and her two colleagues were discussing fundraising initiatives and planning vegetarian menus for their next cooking session. The Leeds branch was formed in 2011 and is run by a dedicated team of volunteers, each of whom give up to three or four hours per week to plan their next session. On cooking days, which take place in a community hall in inner city Leeds once a fortnight, the Hub Leaders are joined by other volunteers who help out throughout the mammoth seven hours it takes to prepare a three course meal for up to ninety regular diners. The Leeds branch work specifically with refugees and asylum seekers and have teamed up with Leeds University group, STAR (Student Action for Refugees) who provide English lessons for those who wish to take them. Lydia told me that much of the food that they use is donated by local supermarkets, and that they don't take meat, fish or dairy products. That way the volunteers are able to cater to a range of ethnic or religious diets and reduce any food safety issues at the same time. The families that dine with Foodcycle are able to take away any excess food at the end of the day, so many go home with enough bread or vegetables to last them for the rest of the week. What struck me about the Foodcycle model is that individual hubs are left to find what fits best in their own communities, as the national organization clearly recognizes what works for one city might not work for another.

Love Food Hate Waste is an initiative set up by the government funded independent waste reduction organization WRAP. As part of its mission to reduce waste and promote recycling across a number of sectors, WRAP set up Love Food Hate Waste in 2007. Working with retailers, Love Food Hate Waste has helped a number of supermarkets to establish their own campaigns directed towards reducing domestic food waste. Sainsbury's 'Love your leftovers' and Morrison's 'Great taste less waste' are two such initiatives, which have contributed a £1.5 billion worth of food saved since the campaign was launched.[8] The website offers a wealth of money and food saving information, with hints and tips on reducing domestic food waste, portion control and better ways to shop for food, together with a plethora of thrifty recipes made with ingredients left over from previous meals. There's no two ways about it, it's a superb initiative, and one from which many can benefit, provided of course that you have an internet connection.

A rapidly expanding model within the food charity sector is that of the 'pay as you feel' (PAYF) café. Customers are fed from menus created entirely from waste food and are invited to leave a donation, rather than a fixed price. In many cases that donation can be in the form of skills, time or expertize rather than hard cash. This pay as you feel approach to food charity borrows directly from the ethos of the food rioters of previous centuries, who gathered at market squares and distributed cart loads of corn amongst their communities on a 'pay as you feel' basis. Clearly in this case it is a 'post market' redistribution, that is to say that the producers and organizations that donate the food to PAYF cafés have already banked their profits and unlike the farmers of the eighteenth and nineteenth centuries they are giving up their produce willingly. To me though, the similarities are too strong to ignore.

I put this to Adam Smith, the founder of the Real Junk Food Project in Armley, Leeds. Adam could see the similarity. He has recently negotiated arrangements with the restaurant chain Nandos, and Morrisons supermarkets and now takes all of their food waste on a daily basis. 'In the beginning we had to go looking for food, but that's now no longer the case', he told me. 'When we were collecting food from supermarket and restaurant bins, it was a bit like the grain redistributions you describe, but it's different now'. Adam went on to tell me that since the arrangement with Morrisons was made public a number of other supermarkets have offered free food to the project. 'We're handling up to three tons of food per week. I'm not interested in taking on other supermarkets' food waste and saving them thousands on landfill and anaerobic digestion taxes. We are even taking food waste from other food charities, we just don't need another supermarket on board at the moment. What we are doing is fundamentally wrong.' Something about Adam's outlook tells me that the Real Junk Food Project is about more than just feeding hungry people, it's about challenging the sanity of the current food system responsible for producing so much waste in the first place. The success of the Real Junk Food model has meant that dozens of new cafés have opened up and down the country, Manchester, Bradford, Brighton, Sheffield and even as far as France, South Africa, Australia and the USA. There's a riot going on.

It's clear that there are an overwhelming number of local and national, community-based initiatives springing up to tackle the problem of food waste, and to re-direct that food into the bellies of hungry people. In this way, by working collectively to help feed others, they all evoke the spirit of food rioters gone by. It's a bold claim, but one I am happy to make, food charity workers are modern day food rioters, it's just that they operate in a manner a little less disruptive than their predecessors. This claim is exemplified through the actions of a remarkable woman I met in February 2015. I described food activist Gill Watson, as a 'one woman food riot'. She laughed out loud, but quickly came round to my way of thinking, and has since set-up a food charity initiative called 'Food Riot Bus'. I explained that Gill's attitude and the way in which she goes about running her one-woman food charity is, in my mind at least, similar to that displayed by the food rioters of the past who helped themselves. Working initially alone and now with just a handful of volunteers and at her own expense, Gill has set up a food aid initiative in the town of Barrowford in Lancashire. Her enthusiasm and the vigour with which she goes about her business has attracted the attention of local and national media, as well as the obvious support of the broader community and those she is seeking to help. Her model is simple, with no small amount of effort, Gill persuaded the manager of her local branch of Lidl supermarket to let her have all of the end of day produce that would otherwise go to waste. This includes perishable goods including bread, fresh fruit and vegetables and on the odd occasion fresh pastries and cakes. Gill collects as much as she can fit into the back of her large four-by-four and deposits the lot in a small wooden shed, which sits outside a local primary school gates. People are encouraged to help themselves, with obvious consideration for others. 'Let them eat cake', laughs Jill, 'and kale, and fresh bread and salad, and whatever else this travesty of a supermarket dominated food system throws up as perfectly good waste.' Gill is angry, but she directs that anger into helping others. Her success has led to part funding from the NHS for her 'Food Riot Bus' initiative.

Tristram Stuart might not necessarily agree of course, but I do think it is appropriate to make the comparison, in fact I would say it is necessary to make the comparison if we are to see the struggle for food as a continuum within a deeply unfair and broken food system. A system which allows the generation of immense wealth for a few, at the expense of the many and one which creates vast mountains of waste food in the process. The notion of collective action, and the amazing and excellent work that Stuart and all of those others do, more often than not in an unpaid capacity, reflects a realization that communities have the capacity to swing the current state of affairs to the benefit of others, and more to the point, people are willing to facilitate that change. It's a common thread that runs through some of the food riots so far examined. In many ways, like in times of old, the government is playing catch-up.

The work of those organizations examined above, all of which are involved in the redistribution of tonnes of waste food to hungry people in this country alone, is growing evidence of ordinary people responding to a growing crisis of food poverty in Britain. It is surely also evidence of a need to re-examine the levels of surplus in the food system. There is even a discrepancy over what to call it, is it food waste or is it 'surplus'? How could there be a surplus of food when people in Britain are going hungry on a daily basis? Yet the insistence is that we need to produce more food if we are all going to have a slice of the pie. To me that's a little like helping yourself to additional roast potatoes when you still haven't finished what's on your plate, I'd call it greedy. Given that the vast majority of surplus food comes from supermarkets, or 'the market' as a whole, it would appear that that is perhaps where the greed lies. It appears that there is an endless queue of willing volunteers (albeit with good intentions) standing in line to help supermarkets tidy up the mess of their inefficient supply chains and over ambitious order books. In fact, the development of food redistribution organizations is currently the fastest growing area within the voluntary sector. You could argue that we are currently witnessing the corporatization of the food charity sector, it's becoming big business. I'm obviously right behind all of those organizations, which redistribute food, but surely there must come a time when we sit back and re-evaluate the present food system. It's what Adam Smith and a number of his colleagues in the food charity sector are driving for. Surely, as in the war years, when food distribution was very much the business of government, there is a role for government to play in making sure people don't go hungry?

In October 2014, the House of Commons Select Committee on Environment, Food and Rural Affairs (EFRA), whose role is to examine the expenditure, administration and policy of the DEFRA, held a session examining the issues of food security, demand, consumption and waste. The committee last looked at food security in 2009, following the food prices spike of 2008. Back then, the Select Committee produced the report, 'Securing Food Supplies up to 2050: the challenges faced by the UK'. It contained a number of recommendations in recognition of the fact that food production must grow rapidly in the light of rising population growth. At the same time, the report recognized that maximizing food production does not depend on agriculture alone but also on infrastructure transport systems, as well as food storage. In a nutshell, distribution of the food we already produce is a key factor. 'Securing Food Supplies' also concluded that food must be affordable to the consumer, but prices must also ensure that food production in the first place remains worthwhile. An agricultural system must be profitable to be healthy.[9] I am not entirely convinced that the recommendations of the report ever found their way into policy decisions over the interim period. Moving forward to October 2014, the Select Committee produced another report, called simply 'Food Security'. It emphasizes the need for 'sustainable intensification' in food production, in other words, more more more. The profitability in the agricultural system mentioned in the 2009 report appears to be geared more towards the employment of technology, rather than addressing the problematic relationship between the farmer and the supermarket buyers, a relationship which clearly gives rise to enormous amounts of food waste in the system. It doesn't take a genius to figure out that the panacea of GM will be up there in the recommendations, and there it is, bullet point number 29 in the conclusions and recommendations, with no reference what so ever about the intellectual property rights connotations of GM production:

> The Government should do more to inform the public about the potential beneficial impacts of growing GM crops in the UK. It should encourage an evidence-led public debate about GM crops and also counter food safety fears about the consumption of GM. In order to give consumers the opportunity to make informed choices, GM foods should be labelled as such, in the same way as organic produce. The Government must continue to work within the EU to argue for a system which is more flexible for those member states that wish to take advantage of GM technology, while still ensuring that all EU consumers are protected, in the same way it does with non-GM technologies. Progress towards this objective must be research and science-led. The Government must also ensure that any GM products grown legitimately in any member state may be freely traded across the EU.

Sadly, Peter Melchet's comments, as the policy director of the Soil Association, which appear on page 40 of the report, don't make it to the final conclusions, he told the committee that Genetic Modification was, 'the product of a narrow, top-down approach, driven not by the needs of farmers, consumers or the environment, but of seed and chemical companies'.

To be fair though, the notion of food waste and surplus distribution was examined by the Select Committee. In its hearing of oral evidence on 22 October 2014, the committee sought the thoughts of food writer and restaurant critic, Jay Rayner and Mark Lineham of the Sustainable Restaurants Association. It also heard evidence from representatives from Morrisons supermarket, as well as Lindsay Boswell and David McCauley, CEOs of Fare Share and the Trussell Trust respectively. The session was televised live on the UK Parliament website, I watched it all. Rayner made the salient point that it might be useful to stop talking about food poverty, and focus on poverty as a whole, and in that respect, the integrity of the committee, or at least the view from the chair, could arguably be summed up by the reply from Anne McIntosh, Conservative MP for Thirsk and Malton, 'If there were more people in work, there would be less people in poverty'. McIntosh clearly had the answers before the session even got going. Unfortunately, the obvious retort about low wages, and how people on low wages are receiving food aid in 2014, was never aired. To me, the committee bore all the signs of a useless confessional, possibly serving merely to feed the egos of those invited to give evidence, rather than a forum in which significant change might be engineered. I say that as a person also having been invited to give evidence in front of a Select Committee on Homelessness back in 2004. I was very pleased, and a little nervous, to have been invited (I even put it on my CV), but I fear that my contribution made not the blindest bit of difference.

A second session, convened on the 29 October 2014, took evidence from Liz Goodwin and Dr Richard Swannell, CEO and Director at WRAP. Maria Ana Neves, CEO of yet another food waste recycling charity, Plan Zheroes was called, as was Tim Smith from Tesco and Nigel Jenny from the Fresh Produce Consortium. Food waste was cited as one of WRAP's top priorities, despite a reduction in budget from the government. Liz Goodwin pointed out that 15 million tonnes of food waste comes from the retail industry, while some 7 million tonnes is generated from households. The committee was keen to learn about perceived cultural barriers to reducing food waste. Maria Ana Neves indicated a need to re-educate the public about wasting food, and offered what she called a controversial step, in suggesting that an increase in food prices might be conducive to lowering the amount of domestic waste. A bold suggestion at a time when affordability appears to be one of the key factors driving people to food banks.

I mentioned earlier what I see as a similarity between the food rioters who were involved in hijacking cart loads of corn in the eighteenth century and re-distributing the produce at affordable prices, and the efforts of the Real Junk Food Project, Plan Zheroes, and Foodcycle and the like. And let it be said that those efforts are commendable, but in a way Tristram Stuart is right in suggesting that such comparisons are inappropriate. The key difference today is that, unlike the unfortunate farmers of years gone by, the supermarkets who are able to willingly give up their waste food for good causes, are fortunate as they have already banked their profits. The food rioters of the past, though an intrinsic part of a broader bargaining process, were operating outside of the market, they had a detrimental effect on farmers' incomes, whereas today's food fighters, by which I mean all of those food charities described above, have been subsumed by the market. Indeed the work that the food redistribution charities does actually contributes to the bottom line of the supermarkets by saving landfill fees. Figures vary, but according to Plan Zheroes, for example, the UK food retail industry sends 1.6 million tonnes of surplus food to landfill every year. If it's going to landfill then we can presumably feel comfortable in calling it what it is, food waste. Any food system which produces that amount of waste must surely be in need of an overhaul. I keep returning to Jay Rayner's paradox of 'supermarkets are evil/supermarkets are not evil', and it's not a debate I really wish to get involved with, as supermarkets are a fact of life and I happen to use them on a regular basis. What I will say is that the practices of supermarket buyers – which in their drive for ever increasing profit margins, hammer down the price paid to farmers and producers to such an extent that significant numbers of farmers are choosing to jack it all in – are questionable to say the least. Such practises clearly run counter to the suggestions of the EFRA Select Committee report of 2009, which held that 'food production in the first place remains worthwhile'. The savings and artificially low prices passed on to the consumer come at a tremendous cost, both to the environment through the growth of agribusiness with its excessive use of artificial fertilizers and swing towards monocultures, to the farmer, and ultimately to the poorest in our societies who can no longer afford to buy the cheap food in the first place. In the light of the struggle that farmers and producers face against supermarket buying power, one could argue that the current food system and the way in which we buy our food presents a classic case of us as consumers, biting the hand that feeds us. Pop will eat itself. Whereas in the past, farmers were often seen by food rioters as 'the enemy' and were often on the direct receiving end of any protests, farmers today are increasingly seen as victims struggling at the hand of the giant supermarkets. More and more farmers are seeking to bypass the power of the supermarket buyers, and turning to direct outlets as a means to secure returns. The mushrooming of Farmers Markets up and down the country must surely be testament to that. Rayner stated clearly in his evidence to the Select Committee that the price of food paid by the consumer must rise if we are to attain a sustainable food system. The Chair of the Select Committee, Anne McIntosh was quick to assert that Rayner appeared to be contradicting himself, given that people are queuing at food banks up and down the country. What Rayner was clearly getting at is the fact that the current system in which farmers receive bottom dollar, while supermarkets accrue huge profits and continue to generate mountains of food waste, is indicative of a broken food system.

This brings with it a not inconsiderable dilemma, as well as what some might easily see as a contradiction. How, at a time when thousands of people in this country are struggling to feed themselves and their families, could we possibly argue for an increase in food prices as an answer? In all honesty, I'm not quite sure, but the answer lies in recognition of the fact that food prices alone are part of a bigger picture. According to DEFRA, in 2012 the average household spend on food stood at 11.6% of income. Significantly, that percentage spend increases for families on lower incomes, rising to 16.6%.[10] The Food Research Collaboration (FRC), a body of academics and civil society organizations, recently (2014) published a key examination of food prices in their briefing paper, UK Food Prices: cooling or bubbling? The report opens with the observation that with the repeal of the Corn Laws in 1846, government policy in the UK has maintained an interest in keeping food prices low as a means of protecting consumers (I would argue that the repeal of the Corn Laws was also implemented as a means of protecting the government at the time too). For two centuries, low food prices have been championed as a benefit to the poor. Clearly any reconsideration of that stance will present a number of potential problems both to governments as well as consumers themselves. It would take a brave captain of a sinking ship to assert that the limited supply of life jackets ought be distributed among the few who were capable of steering the lifeboats. The inference being, of course, that those capable of preserving life be given the means to do so. The FRC paper goes on to examine a number of pitfalls of low food prices and raises the issues of obesity and other chronic diseases which affect those afflicted, as well as the health care system. The paper mentions the impact on farms in the UK, lower food prices can result in a lack of business investment. It points out that demand for cheap food can lead to poor animal management practises and can lead to corners being cut in health protection. The horsemeat scandal of 2013, where some supermarkets chose to substitute cheaper horsemeat for beef in a number of products is a fine example of such. The cultural assumption that 'cheap equals good' must surely be challenged. This is a point alluded to in the second session of evidence heard by the Select Committee in October 2014.

The FRC report concludes in a manner which provokes further inquiry:

> One thing is certain, although there are many in the food sector who would like sensitivities about food prices and affordability to subside, or who think market forces will resolve the matter, the issue is unlikely to fade away. Fundamental pressures in, on and across the UK food system continue to emerge which will keep the issue of food prices bubbling rather than cooling, we suspect.[11]

If we accept that the practise, over the past two centuries, of championing cheap food may have led to the current crisis of food poverty in Britain, as characterized by the rise of food banks and redistribution charities in the recent past, then perhaps we ought to consider food charity as part of the problem rather than a solution. At the very least, it is not too difficult to see that following the present model of redistribution of food waste, and taking it to its logical limit, then there must surely come a time when all of those amazing food charities are in competition with one another, in effect fighting for the scraps left over in the market generated mountain of food waste. The corporatization of food charity is a new area for growth, and supermarkets and the large food companies are keen to get in on the act. The European Federation of Food Banks and the Global Foodbanking Network are at the forefront of assisting communities, the world over, to establish new food banks. The European Federation of Food Banks carries a long list of multinational companies supporting food banks across the world; Kellogg's, Cargill, Unilever, Nestlé, Tesco, together with many others are all key partners in the network. It would be very difficult to argue that the work these organizations are doing is not worth while. I've seen, first hand, that the thousands of volunteers involved are dedicated to relieving food poverty and helping others. At an individual level, their integrity and commitment is beyond reproach, but I can't help thinking that this is a response born of a broken system. It's a return to a residual system of welfare, the epitome of 'trickle down', where people are literally fighting for what amounts to scraps from the table. Dr Graham Riches is Emeritus Professor at the University of British Columbia, in his most recent book, *First World Hunger Revisited* (2014), he argues that the corporatization of food aid offers national governments a way of outsourcing the political risk of domestic hunger.[12] As far back as 2002, Riches was arguing that the rise of voluntary waste food recycling was eroding governments' responsibilities in delivering a right to food. The initiative first described by the United Nations Declaration of Human Rights in 1948, has been left to the inefficiencies of a broken food system and the altruistic efforts of thousands of volunteers to deliver. Whilst we can all feel good about redistributing this mountain of food waste, perhaps we ought be looking for a new food system which doesn't generate waste in the first place. As the Gloucester bread rioters of the eighteenth century sought to interfere with the market in order to ensure an equitable distribution of corn, perhaps the food rioters and protesters of today should follow suit.

Back in 1948, amid a rising tide of collective responsibility, one which owed a lot to the lessons learned through the horror of a recent world war, the newly formed United Nations first described the right to food as part of the right to an adequate standard of living. This notion was strengthened, in 1966, through the International Covenant on Economic, Social and Cultural Rights when the right to food was described as:

> The right to adequate food is realized when every man, woman and child, alone or in community with others, has physical and economic access at all times to adequate food or means for its procurement.

In referring to both physical and economic access to food, the definition encompasses both the production, and distribution of food and accordingly lays down the responsibility for the delivery of those rights at the feet of governments. It was always going to be a difficult right to deliver in the first place, given the fact that the majority of food production worldwide is in the hands of private companies. Whilst clearly enjoying the protection of host governments as well as the international laws governing world trade, private companies of course are not compelled by the proclamations of the United Nations. It is left to the governments of the individual nations which signed up to the Universal Declaration of Human Rights, to determine the degree of control they exert over the free market. In the case of Britain, that control has been on the wain since 1979, and today's rising tide of food poverty is testament to that decline.

END NOTES

1. www.church-poverty.org.uk/foodfuelfinance or from www.oxfam.org.uk/policyandpractice
2. http://www.bbc.co.uk/news/uk-politics-26261700.
3. Trussell Trust, *Information Pack*, 2014.
4. Household Food Security in the UK, Final Report Feb 2014, p.6.

5. Jones, O. *Chavs - the demonization of the working class*, p10.
6. *Daily Mail* Online (www.dailymail.co.uk), published 13 March 2014.
7. FareShare, report and financial statements March 2014.
8. An Introduction to Love Food Hate Waste, WRAP, 2010.
9. 'Securing Food Supplies up to 2050: the challenges faced by the UK.' Stationery Office, London July 2009.
10. DEFRA, 'Family Food Report', 2012.
11. Food Research Collaboration, 'UK Food Prices: cooling or bubbling?', 2014.
12. Riches, G. in Riches & Silvasti (eds). *First World Hunger Revisited*. London, Palgrave Macmillan, 2014. p.202.

CHAPTER TEN

PROTEST AND THE RISE OF THE FOOD HERO

The right to food is the right of every individual, alone or in community with others, to have physical and economic access at all times to sufficient, adequate and culturally acceptable food that is produced and consumed sustainably, preserving access to food for future generations.[1]

In his final report for the United Nations in 2014, outgoing 'special rapporteur on the right to food', Olivier De Schutter concluded that the eradication of hunger and malnutrition is an achievable goal. He noted that empowering communities at the local level in order that they may identify solutions that suit them best is a first step towards that goal. He was of course speaking on a global scale, but his reference to 'community lead' solutions is one that sits well in an historical context. It is the communal capacity for broadcasting and re-affirming the right to food that has often lead to the uprisings covered in these pages. The numbers of participants swelled, as labourers, mill-workers, skilled and unskilled individuals were informed of planned uprisings and action via a network of communication which has evolved and diversified over the ages. From crude posters nailed to church doors, to word of mouth proclamations among labour gangs and gatherings in market squares, word spread among the poor. The loaf on a stick was raised.

As methods of communication developed and increased over the years it became easier to spread the word and to rally others to the cause, though of course the power of the editors, the censors, and later the broadcasters would often act as a counterbalance to spreading the word. The spread of popular protest was aided through the broadside ballads of the eighteenth and nineteenth centuries. Celebrations and laments to the lot of the poor followed suit through folk song and dance, much of which can be seen today through the tradition of folk music and Morris Dance. William Cobbett's lecture tours conducted on his 'rural rides' in the early 1800s, did much to broadcast the state of affairs of the working man, as did his book, *Rural Rides*, which was published with impeccable timing in 1830. We could even argue that many of Charles Dickens' novels brought a degree of protest into the lap of polite society. At the very least, his stories broadcast the lot of the poor in Britain at the time.

Later, as the spread of newspapers began to replace the popular broadsides, people across the country were able to quickly gain a retrospective view of disturbances and food riots. This may have served to re-affirm discontent, or perhaps attract condemnation in equal measure. While researching the chapter on the 'Newlyn Fish Riots', I spent a great deal of time on the British Newspaper Archive website and was struck by just how far and how quickly the news of the riots and trials had spread. Reports appeared in Scottish newspapers, just a day or two after the events, and in regional publications with large coastal communities, where fishy tales would of course be of interest. The reports were often syndicated, but filed none the less. That retrospective view was furthered in the twentieth century, first with the invention of radio and then television. New media platforms enabled campaigners to reach a much broader audience, and in the twenty-first century, the internet and proliferation of social media means that it is now easier than ever to spread the word, to join a campaign, and to register your protest or to support a cause. Modern social media even removes the retrospective, so that participants are able to watch and follow live events as they unfold.

To me, all of this provides a vital and fascinating part of the story of *Food Worth Fighting For*. Before I threw myself into the research for this book, I had no idea of the extent to which hungry people in the past would go to further their cause. I had no idea that our history is peppered with food riots, and it is thanks largely to some of the texts cited within this chapter of the story that this knowledge remains, and that to me is important. Through the evolution of popular protest, we often find heroes coming to the fore, food heroes, leaders, rebels, who through their efforts and those of their companions have bettered the lot of others. So this chapter is a celebration of those food heroes of the past and the present.

> The English rebel may only rarely be a triumphant one or even a particularly likeable character. But he and she are as much a part of the fabric of English history as the monarchs, law-makers and political leaders they defied. They serve as an inspiration, as warning, and sometimes simply as example. They may not always be visible, but they, too, are all around us.[2]

'Visibility' of course depends greatly on the ability to communicate, as well as the ability to use the means of communication available at the time. Popular protest is important in any campaign, it's a means of swelling the ranks of your supporters and amplifying the voice. Sadly though, much of the research into food riots, particularly in the recent past, does little in terms of exploring the protestor voice. Explanations of food riots are very often described as a series of actions, which occur as a response to the mechanics of price in an emerging or changing market, or as a reaction to other structural changes. Whilst this may indeed often be a determining factor of food riots and protest, and of course highly relevant, I fear that in adopting such a reductionist approach, the human side of food fights is lost. Accordingly any lessons learned through the broader description of a social landscape in these conflicts, can become obscured. It is important to remember that even in a crowd with a common aim, people will behave and interact with their surroundings in different ways. Many of us, for example, would think little of tossing a few coins into a collection bucket, or displaying a sticker in the back window of a car. But few would dare to face down the might of the Russian naval fleet in the Arctic, or scale the heights of London's tallest building to unfurl a banner. The age of pressure group politics is with us, and you don't necessarily have to be at the coal (not Dole) face to participate. In 1991, I joined the ranks of some 100,000 protestors on the streets of San Francisco, voicing opposition to the Gulf War. I'd seen handbills and posters advertizing the coming protest and was swept along by the communal feeling of camaraderie. I have to admit that I was somewhat confused by the mass chant of my immediate comrades, 'We're here, we're queer, we're not going shopping!' but I felt a sense of overall belonging as we marched in our tens of thousands down Market Street towards the downtown area of the city and caused the shut down of the Bay Bridge.

To return to an age where literacy rates were a fraction of what they are today, recruitment to a popular cause relied more heavily on word of mouth and the actions of communities bound together under a popular motif. 'We'd rather be hanged than starve to death' was a cry which rang out among the Ely and Littleport rioters in 1816. The actions of a whole community were stirred by an initial meeting of members of a benefit club. No handbills or posters went out, just a word of mouth swelling of protest and anger. The outcome of those riots brought terrible consequences for some. John Dennis, William Beamiss the elder, Isaac Harley, Thomas South and George Crow were unfortunate in being picked out from among the scores of rioters arrested and tried at the special assizes in Ely. They paid for their actions, and died repentant, on the gallows in the town of Ely in 1816. Though not seen as heroes at the time, their actions and those of their colleagues are celebrated today in the costume and dance of 'El Riot' as mentioned earlier – the Ely & Littleport Riot Fenland Morris Side based in Ely. The multicoloured waistcoats, black skirts and red handkerchiefs that the dancers wear reflect Fenland individuality, the black peat Fenland soils, and the spirit of bloody revolt. Through popular culture, the Bread and Beer Riots are remembered today.

The Broadside Ballad came to be an important way of spreading news, of celebrating military triumphs and passing comment on society and politics, as well as marking the signs of the times. Printed on a single sheet, and sometimes illustrated with woodcut images, broadsides were often sold by vendors in the street and carried popular themes to the masses. Their balladic meter and assonance made them easier to learn by ear, and meant that those unable to read were able to repeat them, having heard them read aloud in public houses and market squares. Douglas Jerrold, a journalist writing for the satirical magazine *Punch* during the 1840s, referred to broadsides as 'half penny historical abridgements – narrow strips of history that adorned the garrets of the poor'.[3] In fact, the broadsides had a wider appeal and were frequently portrayed by artists such as Hogarth in popular street scenes of the 1800s. Covering a broad gamut of subject matter, the broadsides could be said to reflect the word on the street. Music historian Roy Palmer described the ballads 'as a means of self-expression ... an art form truly in the idiom of the people'.[4] That broadsides were used as tools of dissent is clear, as governments over the years have often sought to ban them on occasions when they touched a raw nerve, inflicting harsh penalties for those that dared to defy the bans. It is a medium that, despite the disappearance of printed broadsides towards the end of the nineteenth century, has long-served counter cultures and protest movements the world over. In the 1960s, Bob Dylan sang the 'The Times They Are A Changin'.'[ ] I suspect that the conditions hadn't changed all that much since the 1820s, when a broadside balladeer at the time declared that 'The Times Have Altered' – 'Come all you swaggering farmers, whoever you may be, One moment pay attention and listen to me.'[5] The use of music and song to further a cause enables a broader community to join in and voice support, even though they may not necessarily be at the centre of the action.

Fortunately for historians, and those with a passing interest, the words of the balladeers capture a sense of the times. One gets a first hand account, described in the vernacular language of the period. They help paint a detailed picture and, in some cases, describe a world which unfortunately in many ways resembles our world today. But most of all, we are given a lasting record of periods in history when times were hard, an ancient form of social media recorded or written down for posterity and safeguarded in the collections of famous collectors of song and verse, like Cecil Sharp and Percy Grainger. We often talk of history repeating itself, but the ballads written down sometimes seem to indicate a continuation, rather than a cycle of repetition. It seems Bob Dylan was wrong, the times are not changing at all. They seem to have altered little since these words ran from the tongues of those who sang them in the mid nineteenth century. Though in this case, the war to which the author refers here is the Crimean War, the conditions described could just have easily be applied to the Seven Years War, which ended in 1763, and would be familiar to the food rioters of 1776.

There never was such hard times seen in England before

Good people all, both great and small, come listen to my rhymes,
I'll sing to you a verse or two, concerning of the times;
The butchers and the bakers they've come to one decision,
With the millers and the Quakers on the prices of provision.

Chorus
There never was such hard times seen in England before.
The man who speculates in corn will purchase all he can,
He's nothing but a traitor to the honest working man;
And I am sure before the poor should have it under price;
He'd leave it in his granary for all the rats and mice.

They talk about Free Trade, my boys, but that is all my eye,

Their fortune it is made and banked, we may lie down and die;
We need not look for honesty among a lot of elves,
Free Trade is but a policy, they have it all themselves.

The farmers whistle Charley, we had some splendid crops:
Oats, taters, wheat and barley, and lots of turnip tops;
They seem to say, 'Good lack-a-day, success attend the Czar':
They're making money every day all by the Russian war.

The farmers, millers, bakers too, are plucking up their feathers,
They are a mob, so help me Bob, of humbugs all together;
The bounteous gifts of Providence, they do monopolise,
And rob the poor, I'm certain sure, their guts to gourmandize.

If I'd my way, mark what I say, I'd screw their bellies tight,
I'd send them off to Russia and make the tigers fight;
Sad would be their condition, they'd carry, oh dear oh lack,
Full seventy rounds of ammunition, stuck on the landlord's back.

Now go into a shambles, there's mutton and beef enough,
At seven pence a pound, you'll find it rather tough;
Come buy, come buy, it is the cry, resounds from stall to stall,
But when you come to eat it, keep your napper from the wall.

The pawn shops they are crowded out with different kinds of things:
Shawls, petticoats and trousers and ladies' wedding rings,
The landlord and landlady too, are looking fat and plump,
With her crochet knitted night cap and bustle on her rump.

The Cotton Lords of Lancashire, they think it is no more;
They say, be dad, the trade is bad, and they must have short time;
They eat their beef and mutton, eye, and sport about on Monday,
But they do not care a button if you eat brick on Sunday.[6]

The resentment and animosity towards the speculators and food
producers in this ballad, which actually dates from around 1854, is
clear to see. This is not just an observation of 'shocking hard times',

this is an overt criticism of the free market and the development of capitalism. It's clear that the farmers, butchers and bakers are seen as being in cahoots. Social criticism was a popular theme of the broadside ballad, although the authorities also sought to use their popularity to advantage too. The popular ballad, 'The Riot – half a loaf is better than no bread', which was described in the introduction to this book, is an example of such. The earliest printed ballads date back to the early 1500s, but as competition from newspapers began to bite, the tradition of the street balladeers waned. In the introduction to their 1957 collection of ballads, *The Common Muse*, Allan Rodway and Vivian De Sola Pinto note that by the early Victorian period, the ballad-monger had became a pitiable figure, living on tips from better class people who remember him from palmier days than on the proceeds of his sales. Ballads were used not just as a means of criticism, but often as a means of recording events with pride; they form what Roy Palmer calls 'the sound of history'. Those early sounds have become muted in some cases, lost, buried or forgotten over time.

That the mythical character Captain Swing, (outlined in chapter three), is still celebrated as a hero in the works of modern songwriters is testament to the spirit of protest, with verses to his actions still being penned over a century and a half since he lit the skies over southern England. A more likely candidate for a 'food hero' award at the time however, would be the political reformist and champion of the poor, William Cobbett. For me at least, William Cobbett is Captain Swing personified. He was a food hero in more ways than one. As a farmer he was concerned with the quality of his produce, publishing his *Cottage Economy* in 1822. *Cottage Economy* was a book dedicated to instruction on bread making, bee keeping and beer brewing, a tome that Tom and Barbara Good (from *The Good Life)* would no doubt have consulted had it been in print in the 1970s. It served as a manual for the farm labourer in the early nineteenth century, though of course crippling taxes on corn, sugar and malt at the time meant that his instructions were in many ways lost on his target audience. He experimented with cross breeding crops and introduced his own strain of maize, which he somewhat rather vainly named 'Cobbett's Corn' to the English countryside. In my mind though, it was his actions on his famed series of 'rural rides' which set out his stall as a food hero. Travelling through the southern counties of England, he set out to 'enlarge the radical platform of the countryside.'[7] Through his series of lectures, Cobbett spread word of the plight of the rural labourer, and no doubt emboldened many of the Swing rioters into action. From this perspective, the changes to the Poor Laws which followed not long after the riots, could be seen as having been prompted by the actions of William Cobbett. For Cobbett himself, his vociferous championing of the farm labourer led to a trial for seditious libel. There are clearly risks associated with standing up and voicing concerns.

By the mid nineteenth century, food related public unrest and popular uprising was embedded in the fabric of British society. Food rioters were beginning to see the results of their labours despite the efforts of the authorities to quell the disturbances using the full weight of the law. As we have seen, the 'Swing Riots' prompted a re-examination of the Poor Laws at the time. The old accepted view that food riots were a mere pressure valve through which anger of the poor might be vented were beginning to be more closely examined in satirical magazines. *Punch* was first published in 1841 and a similar publication *Fun* followed twenty years later. Both carried cartoons lampooning politicians of the time, as wells campaigners and reformers, and served to embed popular protest within literary society. Satirical attacks on leaders, heroes and villains have long proved popular among the public. In a way, they are even easier to access than lengthy balladic tomes which repeatedly decry the lot of the poor.

Food heroes and champions are often inadvertently preserved, presented and held aloft through the process of popular protest. Named in song and depicted in cartoon, they are introduced to a broader public for either derision or admiration. 'Old King Cole was an angry old soul, and an angry old soul was he: he didn't approve of the Beverage bowl and he called it fiddle-de-de', was a caption that appeared in *Punch* magazine in 1942 below a cartoon image of William Beverage. An unsung food hero, Beverage's work on *British Food Control*, published in 1928, presented a detailed account of the efficacy of government intervention in the food chain and the market. Though clearly focusing on a time of crisis as Britain entered the First World War, Beverage's work highlighted the benefits of an organized food control system in tackling food queues and suppressing dissent and unrest in times of national shortage. His observations highlighted the shortfalls of the free market system in dealing with crisis and allaying the fears of a hungry population. Penned originally as a summary of 'lessons learned' in a time of rationing, many of those lessons were then incorporated into the rationing system adopted by Churchill's government during the Second World War. In his closing remarks, he observed that rationing was 'in effect demanded by the public, long before the government could be got to decide that it was necessary.'[8] A rare and clear cut example of the benefits of a government seeing the benefits of actually listening to its electorate. Beverage, of course, went on to pen a much more important and influential document in 1942. The 'Beverage Report' as it is know was one of the documents that arguably paved the way for the creation of the welfare state which we know today.

The Second World War went on to produce a number of unlikely food heroes. Despite his death in tragic circumstances in 1952, Professor Jack Drummond was also an unwitting food hero of his time. Through his pioneering work, and that of his wife and colleague Anne Wilbraham, the science of nutrition was brought into the day-to-day business of government. Drummond's expertize was used to inform the dietary requirements of rations, not just for soldiers on active duty, but also for the population who remained at home. His book, *The Englishman's Food* (first published in 1939), was a detailed study of the English diet through five centuries. Beginning in Tudor England, Drummond noted the detrimental impact that the Enclosure Movement had on the diet of ordinary citizens, as early enclosures were carried out creating grazing for sheep. It was the wool, rather than the mutton that was the prize at the time. With observations on scurvy, rickets and vitamin deficiencies through the ages, this is one of the first books to look in detail at the relationship between a balanced diet and human health. After the Second World

War, Jack Drummond was appointed as nutritional advisor to the British Control Commission in defeated Germany. He was involved in organizing special feeding programmes for the starving in the newly liberated cities of the Netherlands, as well as the survivors of a number of concentration camps.

In 1941, Dr Carrot and Potato Pete joined the war effort, doing their bit for king and country. An unlikely, but arguably highly effective, pair of food heroes they were cartoon characters devised by the Ministry of Food in a bid to educate the British public as to the nutritional value of tubers and root vegetables. Dr Carrot appeared first, an erudite character complete with top hat, cane and doctor's bag with 'Vit A' emblazoned on the side. Potato Pete followed shortly. A more down to earth character with a jaunty hat, big boots and spats. Pete even came with his own song:

> Here's the man who ploughs the fields. Here's the girl who lifts up the yield. Here's the man who deals with the clamp, so that millions of jaws can chew and champ. That's the story and here's the star, Potato Pete eat up, ta ta!

Between them, they brought home the importance of using up every scrap of food in the pantry, while opening eyes to the nutritional value of our food. Evelyn Balfour took steps a little further in her work on the benefits of organic farming. At a time when new aggro-chemicals were being scattered across the land, Balfour prevented the baby being thrown out with the bathwater. Her scepticism and concerns with modern agricultural practices led to a re-evaluation and a revisiting of the farming methods of old, and the eventual setting-up of the Soil Association, an organization still very active in the food fights of today.

These people were key figures which appeared in the public view at significant waypoints in the development of the food system which we have today. Each gave pause for thought and offered new alternatives and fresh information, not just for the end consumer, but for governments too along the way. Their efforts can be seen to have shaped and influenced, not just the food system, but in some cases the development of the welfare state, raising peoples' awareness, appealing to broader audiences and enticing them to participate and seek change to the status quo. Things, of course, changed greatly following the Second World War. It was not long after that that the ancient practise of gleaning died out in the English countryside.

This gleaning song, sung by Clifford Yeldham, an Essex Morris man, was first written down in 1958, and comes from the collection of Russell Wortley, held in the British Library. It describes the gathering of a few scattered ears of corn, and perhaps hints at the dwindling practise of gleaning as 'poor Mary' is compelled to work all day in the field while others have 'left off'.

'The Gleaner'

Just before the bright sun rises over the hill
In a cornfield poor Mary was seen
Impatient her little own apron to fill
With a few scattered ears she must glean

She never leaves off to run off from her place
For to play or to idle or chat
Except now and then just to wipe her hot face
And to fan herself with a broad hat

Poor girl hard at work in the heat of the sun
How weary and tired she must be
Why don't she leave off as the others have done
And go'nd sit with them under the tree

Oh no for her mother lies ill in her bed
Too feeble to spin or to knit
Her poor little brothers are crying to bread
And yet she can't give them a bit

So how can I be merry and idle and play
While they are so hungry and ill
Oh no for I'd rather work hard all the day
My little blue apron to fill

And then I go home with my heart full of glee
As bright as the lark in the morn
How pleased will my mother and brothers then be
When they see I've a lap full of corn[9]

Without this and other songs and ballads, we would be missing out on, certainly what I see as a key element in historical food protest, and one that once recorded or written down will continue to amplify the protestor voice and provide a broader 'social' context to conditions under which food rioters and food fighters went about their business. It is clear that food riots and protest emerged as a response to a number of factors, and not just rising prices. What is also clear, as historians Alun Howkins and Ian Dyck have pointed out in the journal, *History Workshop*,[10] is that many, if not all of the songs which come forward from the times, are strong on description of 'shocking hard times', but offer little by way of a solution, or to use their words many of the ballads are, 'inarticulate on politics if eloquent on problems'.

But protest in this day and age need not be restricted to song and verse alone. Would be food heroes and campaigners were given a tremendous boost with the advent of television. As the popularity of this new media spread following the Second World War, cookery programmes followed suit. In 1946, Britain laid eyes on its first TV 'celebrity chef', Philip Harben. Harben's television programme, *Cookery* was in many ways, an extension of the efforts of the Ministry of Food's drive to educate and encourage the population to prosper nutritionally under rationing. In more recent years, food programmes on television have evolved from their solely didactic role, offering know how and advice on cookery. Within the past few years, television has provided a platform for celebrity chefs and campaigners such as Jamie Oliver and Hugh Fearnley-Whittingstall, both of whom have had a major impact on the viewing public. Their high profile campaigns have attracted huge numbers of followers and subscribers, both at home and abroad. Oliver's efforts at revolutionizing school dinners in the United Kingdom turned him into an all-out food revolutionary, the epitome of the modern day food rioter. He went on to set up his own charitable foundation, which runs the 'Ministry of Food', campaign, mimicking the efforts of the wartime British government department in educating people about balanced diets and cooking with fresh ingredients. Hugh Fearnley-Whittingstall's campaign, 'Hugh's Fish Fight', launched in 2010 then later abbreviated to 'Fish Fight', attracted a staggering 850,000 supports from 195 different countries and lead to a change in the law as the European Parliament voted to ban the discarding of healthy fish in February 2013. Hugh's campaign highlighted the fact that half the fish caught in the North Sea was being thrown back overboard dead, due to the current quota system which has come about through the current EU Common Fisheries Policy. More recently Hugh has taken up the cause in terms of tackling food waste through another televised campaign which is airing as I type these words. As Hugh's current campaign brings many of the projects, organizations and individuals reported in these pages to the small screen, perhaps for the first time, a TV viewing nation will become aware of the madness in our current food system.

The power of celebrity in rallying a campaign is clear, but those food heroes I've identified prior to Jamie and Hugh were not in themselves celebrities per se. Each sought to further their work and their campaigns using means available at the time. Similarly today, food campaigners sitting way below the celebrity radar are hard at work furthering the cause of sanity in the food system. All of those people mentioned in the previous chapter on food poverty, those involved in the re-distribution of waste food, Paddy and Carol Henderson who set up the Trussell Trust, Tristram Stuart, Kelvin Cheung, Lindsay Boswell among many others, are working with the tools available to hand. Adam Smith and Gill Watson, each with a different and unconventional approach to their work, are both openly critical of not only the food system as a whole, but also directly critical of some of the commercial enterprises they are working with. Thanks to the internet and the development of new social media like Facebook and Twitter, food heroes such as these are able to attract others to their campaigns. We've come a long way from the proclamations nailed to church doors and broadside ballads, it's the internet which enables food fighters to gather en-masse and take action. The thousands of gleaners, the food recyclers, the volunteers at food banks and community shops are all food heroes, modern day food rioters if you like, calling for change and working to ensure that people don't go hungry in our modern society. They are a part of the fabric of British history.

What is surprising then is, with the exception of the period in 1917, when large numbers of people took to the streets in search of food and the government took control of the food system through rationing as well as through production, we have not witnessed all out food rioting on the streets of Britain for over a hundred years. Apart from a few scuffles in Hyde Park at the end of the affair, even the hunger marches of the inter-war years also passed relatively peacefully. I contacted Naomi Hossain, Research Fellow at the Institute of Development Studies, and co-author of 'Them Belly Full (But We Hungry', a fascinating report which looked at Food rights struggles in Bangladesh, India, Kenya and Mozambique (2014). I was curious as to why, whilst food riots have taken place in other parts of the world, we have not witnessed such in Britain for many many years. Naomi's reply raised a number of interesting points. 'In a way', she told me, 'food banks tell us all we need to know, the economic system is so fundamentally flawed that large numbers of citizens accept the stigma of charity and are left with little option but to accept help in the form of food aid.' She went on to say that people in the UK have been able to cope for a long time with higher food prices, as well as the fact that, today, hungry people are coming together at the food bank, where they are recipients of charity, they do not convene at the factory or in the markets or other places where the spatial and group characteristics might enable people to mobilize. That ability to cope is supported with a welfare benefits system, which is now under severe attack and is likely to disappear completely. In truth, Britain has witnessed mass demonstration in recent years, in numbers which far exceeded those of the inter-war hunger marches. Recent protest has been directed towards austerity cuts, in March 2011, some 250,000 people took to the streets of London, again in 2012 some 150,000 protestors marched through the streets of the capital, while others marched in Glasgow and Belfast. In June 2014 50,000 people took part in further anti austerity demonstrations. The numbers are clearly there, but the focus is on a broader call. I raised the question again more recently at the launch of the 'Hungry for Change' report at the Houses of Parliament. I asked the commission whether in the light of excessive cuts to welfare, members thought we might see food riots on the streets of Britain in the near future. Again the response was in the negative as recipients of food charity were deemed to be too embarrassed to riot or kick up a fuss. I'm not sure I agree with that observation. It can't be too long before the sheer numbers of recipients of food charity serves as an indicator to the rest of the population that the system is broken. It might not be just the poor and destitute that kick up a fuss. Once people realize that, as Adam Smith says, 'The Real Junkfood Project doesn't just feed poor people, we're here to feed everybody', then the current market model is in for a bit of a shock.

The fact that the focus of recent anti-austerity marches has been on the economic system, rather than a specific focus on the food system and food poverty per se is due to food poverty being rooted in poverty itself. Perhaps Jay Rayner was right in suggesting to the select committee that we ought drop 'food' and talk about poverty as a whole. Indeed a key finding or suggestion of the 'Hungry for Change' report was that food insecurity ought best be tackled by increasing incomes.

The siege-bound welfare state is clearly being backed-up today, through charitable food aid provision and all the while that food aid is available to the poor, then the easier it is for government to slip more restrictions and welfare cuts through parliament. The fact that food aid is left for charities to provide, strengthens the argument that the government is indeed, as Graham Riches would say, outsourcing the political risk of domestic hunger. Food charities themselves are determined to remain outside of the welfare state, as Chris Mould, CEO of the Trussell Trust has stated, 'Our volunteers will say: "I didn't volunteer to work for the government, I volunteered because I want to help".'[11] The sheer numbers of volunteers working for food charities (the Trussell Trust alone has around 30,000) would suggest that people do indeed want to help. Staggered by the number of volunteers working for the Trussell Trust, I looked a little further in to the numbers of people working for other food charities. Surprisingly, not all of the food charities have this information to hand, so a whole afternoon and in the region of 50 phone conversations with various food charities and a similar number of emails later, I arrived at a working figure of 40,000. It's an approximate figure obviously, but 40,000 volunteers is a sizeable workforce. It happens to be a workforce similar in size to that of Mitchells and Butlers, the UK's largest operator of restaurants, pubs and bars. That's irony right there. Their brands; Harvester, Toby Carvery and All Bar One, to name just three are familiar up and down the country. Obviously Mitchells and Butlers' have to pay for their ingredients as well as their workforce, and their customers are actually paying for the food that they consume, but the company made a before-tax profit of £123 million on the 130 million meals they served in 2014. There is a similar workforce of up to 40,000 individuals out there, working for free in a sub market providing food aid up and down the country. It beggars belief.

As I have suggested, this throng of willing volunteers giving up their time to help prevent others going hungry, is in my mind symbolic of the determination of those rioters in the past who marched on markets and took direct action. It represents a rise in popular protest today, a mobilization of those wanting to make food available, but what is perhaps worthy of note, is that it does not appear to be the 'poor and hungry' themselves (i.e. the recipients of food aid) that are 'rioting'. Of course, during my research, food charity workers and mangers told me how the ranks of their volunteers were swelled by previous recipients of food aid joining in to help out and 'put something back', but by and large volunteers were made up of those often in work who gave up their spare time. To what end, I'm not sure, but this made me think of the lengths that magistrates would go to in demonstrating that those who stood accused of riot in the docks before them were not destitute, but were in employment.

END NOTES

1. Report of the Special Rapporteur on the right to food, Olivier De Schutter: Final report: 'The transformative potential of the right to food', p3.
2. Horspool, D. *The English Rebel.*
3. Cited in Palmer, R. *A Touch of the Times*, p8.
4. Palmer, R. *A Touch of the Times*, p18.
5. The opening lines to 'The Times Have Altered', cited in Rodway & Sola Pinto, *The Common Muse.*
6. 'What shocking hard times', cited in Palmer, R. *A Touch of the Times*, p223-224.
7. Ian Dyck, in the introduction to the Penguin edition of Cobbett's *Rural Rides*, 2001.
8. Beverage. W. *British Food Control*, p.230.
9. 'The Gleaner', first recorded in 1958, from the Russell Wortley collection held in the British Library.
10. Howkins, A and Dyck, I: 'The Time's Alteration': *Popular Ballads, Rural Radicalism and William Cobbett, History Workshop, xxiii/1* (1987).
11. Cited in an article by Patrick Butler in the *Guardian*, 'Chris Mould, social entrepreneur; a question of responsibility', 18 September 2012.

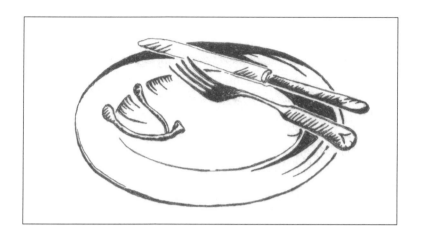

CONCLUSION

Just as an impending food riot – a call for the just and equal distribution of food among the poor – was once signified by the raising of a loaf on a stick, it is fair to say that the food system we have in Britain today, was itself, largely shaped by loaves and sticks. The 'parish loaf', relief doled out to the poor, was backed up by the 'stick' of the law, the riot act. Food riots made a difference. They brought significant gains for many of the participants at the time, as well as setting in train benefits in future years. They paved the way for the creation of the welfare state. Throughout this book, I have deliberately used the terms 'food riot' and 'food fight' side by side, I see them as interchangeable terms, which describe the centuries old struggle, both to put food on the table and achieve, or regain, balance in the prevailing food system. Food riots have often emerged as a response to price rises, poverty and hunger, and to the development of technology, but in addition to this, food riots owe much to a common set of beliefs and ideals among the communities from which they emerge. 'Rough music' was metered out to influential individuals, farmers, millers, cheesemongers, bakers and magistrates. In Cornwall, the focus of frustration was directed against the Sabbath breakers, those who would interfere with the 'moral economy'. Throughout the centuries, hungry crowds sought to tip the scales of injustice, taking direct action to achieve their goals. Food riots also erupted as a response to the policy decisions and actions of successive governments over the years. Elements of Thompson's 'moral economy' have combined with Bohstedt's notion of 'provision politics' as communities, as well as governments, have set about bettering their own circumstances. At the time, prosecuting authorities went to great lengths to demonstrate that those brought before the court were far from destitute in an attempt to portray their actions as those born of avarice and wanton violence and destruction, rather than of poverty and want. Early food riots were the actions of the fiscally poor, but alongside affluent citizens, who took into battle their morals, armed with a sense of what is right, a 'common sense' if you like. I believe that the same energy and a not dissimilar 'moral economy' is prevalent among those today who become involved in food charity, either as volunteers, or as professionals, the pioneers setting-up new programmes and projects. They see injustice in the prevailing food and economic systems, and choose to do something about it. In twenty-first century Britain, it is not necessarily the poor themselves who gather together to take direct action, rather it is others who choose to act on their behalf, drawn by a common need to contribute to the 'common good'. What is interesting is that the market is apparently engaged in a game of catch-up, as supermarkets queue up to hand over their waste produce to the emerging industry of food charities. Capitalism is cashing-in on that feel-good factor that is associated with helping others less fortunate than oneself. The corporatization of food charity is already well under way. The danger is that, as supermarkets find a convenient and low cost way to dispose of their waste produce, then the impetus for re-examining the broken, inefficient and divisive food system which leads to such over production and waste in the first place, will be lost. That is of course until campaigners such as Adam Smith and others withdraw their services and the supermarkets are once again left facing enormous landfill bills which eat into their bottom line.

The nature of the riot has changed, as have the prevailing economic circumstances in which it takes place. The goal, however, i.e. the desire of communities for a just, equitable and affordable distribution of food, remains firmly in place. The Universal Declaration of Human Rights and its subsequent qualifications, has reiterated and reaffirmed a right to food for all. In the twenty-first century, in Britain at least, the food riot is re-invented as a struggle, a 'food fight', and it is a fight that is far from settled. It's an on-going and iterative phenomenon, which is likely to develop in different ways as other factors such as climate change and population growth continue to place strain on the present food system. The marked increase in numbers using food banks and other forms of food charity is testament to this. For me, the constant government denial of, or refusal to see, any link between welfare reform and the growing queues for food charity today, mirrors those efforts of magistrates in the past who, by repeatedly referring to offenders' incomes were also in a way making a similar denial. If the food rioters of the past could be portrayed as acting through a tendency to violence, rather than as hungry citizens in need of help, then the authorities are in a way absolved of any obligation to ameliorate the circumstances of the poor. Today, as the government refuses to acknowledge the most significant cause of referrals to food aid in Britain (falling incomes and an all out attack on the welfare state and sanctioning of benefits), those who find themselves queuing at food banks are portrayed as feckless individuals, solely responsible for their own predicament. According to the government as well as a mis-informed and, in my mind, gullible proportion of the country's population, they deserve what they get.

As I set out to research this topic, I initially wanted to find out what went wrong, convinced as I am, that a million people reliant on food aid in Britain today is an unacceptable wrong in this day and age. What I see now is that it has been 'wrong' for a very long period of time. I'm not even sure that it ever was 'right', but people have been willing to stand up and challenge the status quo over the years, as successive governments introduced legislation which exacerbated the suffering of the poor. For me, an obvious extension of that wrong was the development and expansion of the Acts of Enclosure. Way back in the sixteenth century, when commoners began to loose the capacity to grow and graze their own food, while insufficient compensatory measures were put in place by those that took away their livelihood, that was when the seeds of the food riot were sewn.

Consequently, as the pressure of poverty and hunger in the countryside grew to such an extent that practically the whole of southern England was alight with rage, the government initially sought to point the finger at avaricious 'middle men'. As discontent spread and prevailed, resulting in increasing damage to property, and began to pose a threat to the establishment, successive governments at the time clamped down heavily on food rioters. Some relief was given as poor law reform took shape in the nineteenth century and a marked, or inferred admission of the link between hunger and social unrest was admitted by the allocation of some allotment land to the poor. It was little, and proved barely adequate to stem the feelings of injustice, let alone stem the hunger of the poor.

Things appeared to get better for a short while in the twentieth century, during and after the Second World War, in a period when the country attempted to 'pull together' in the face of a common enemy, but in more recent times that short lived progress has receded. We seem to have reverted to a political and economic climate in which enclosure can prosper once more. Up until the eighteenth century, localized food riots were seen by the government as an acceptable consequence of the unequal distribution of wealth. They acted as a pressure valve through which the poor were able to vent their frustrations by controlling prices in the market. It wasn't until those frustrations erupted into the 'Swing Riots' which spread rapidly across much of southern England, that the government sought to remove that valve and replace it with Poor Law reform and a marginal increase in welfare provision. Today that pressure valve is once more in play, through the efforts of those food fighters providing food charity to people in need. The irony is that the well intentioned efforts of the modern day food fighters are merely serving to preserve the status quo and inadvertently facilitating an all out assault on the poor. The proliferation of food charity in Britain today relieves pressure on the government as it makes swathing cuts in welfare, and blunders head-on towards a political landscape which would be familiar to many of the food rioters noted in this book. The sheer arrogance (it can't possibly be ignorance can it?) of our political leaders, through denial of poverty and a persistent denial of the link between poverty and hunger, is in train with the arrogance of the government and establishment back in the eighteenth century. Back then the market, the free market, freed from public intervention by the reading of the Riot Act, before any relief on taxes and tariffs was considered, was seen as the answer. So too today the free market is expected to provide. Supermarkets unload their mountains of waste, mountains produced by an inefficient, exploitative production model which is geared solely to maximize profits and produce dividends for shareholders, rather than any altruistic desire to 'feed the world'. Its as though we are travelling backwards in time, cutbacks in welfare are increasingly leading to the spread of food poverty and the government seems happy to let the market and the emerging sub market of food aid once more provide the solution.

It seems to me that it was the actions of food rioters in the past that inadvertently gave rise to the notion of the free market we have today. To many, a free market sounds so much more positive than a controlled market, which brings inherent connotations of imprisonment and restriction. We all love our freedom, surely. What strikes me, is that before the market could be freed from any fiscal legislation and restrictions imposed by a government, it was initially freed from the pesky interference from a disgruntled public. As successive waves of rioters descended upon markets across the country in 1776, fixing prices that they and their companions could better afford, the government set about 'freeing the market' by reading the riot act and metering out severe punishments to those who would interfere. By the nineteenth century, as food riots were put down and dealt with increasingly swiftly, the markets were indeed 'free' from intervention from price setting by an aggrieved and hungry public. The Corn Laws which were introduced in 1815 established a government imposed restriction on the market, but that was finally removed some twenty-five years later at the behest of the industrialists.

I have argued that the intentions of some of the food rioters in the past are reflected in the actions of those who provide food charity today, but there is a significant difference in those actions. The Gloucester bread rioters, and all those others who sought to improve their own circumstances and those of the poor, were operating outside of the market. In the intervening years, the freedom of the market has been protected to such a degree that modern food fighters are compelled to operate within it, and to this end, the market is triumphant. It is difficult to make these observations without appearing to demean the efforts of the food charity workers of today, but food charity is very much provided within the realms of the market. In fact it is due entirely to the operation of the market that mountains of food waste accrue; produce left to rot in the fields purely for aesthetic reasons being an excellent example. As I mentioned earlier, the supermarkets, from which the lion's share of food aid comes, have already banked their profits. The market is thus able to recuperate and embrace any notion of rebellion or direct action, in fact it welcomes it. By getting directly involved in, and supporting food aid with the 'recycling' of food waste, supermarkets and the giant food companies are able to enjoy huge savings on what would otherwise be an enormous landfill bill. What is more, they are also able to claim a 'community dividend' as they are seen as 'doing their bit for community' at the same time. That way, we can all feel good. But can we? How can we feel good about a food system that generates such waste in the first place and relies on volunteers to distribute that waste among the poor in a sub-market, one which is associated with shame and failure and lays that blame at the feet of those in the queue for food. And with that comes a wholly familiar framework of language, one which is employed as readily today as it was back in the nineteenth century; the notion of the 'undeserving poor'. It's a theme that Owen Jones picks up on in his book, *Chavs*, as he points out that, 'smearing poorer working class people as idle, bigoted, uncouth and dirty makes it more and more difficult to empathise with them'.[1] Just as magistrates and judges cast aspersions over those who stood before them in the dock in previous years, politicians and media commentators today appear willing, even eager, in their assertions that the poor today are feckless victims of their own actions and decisions.

It's not just the language of the past which is seemingly making a comeback, but legislation too. I talked of the enclosure movements sowing the seeds of food riots in this country. Somewhat ironically today, it is seeds themselves, which have become subject to enclosure, through expansion of Intellectual Property rights protection. The scope for further expansion of the enclosures is ushered in with the promotion of genetic modification and the protection of intellectual property rights. As GM is increasingly pushed as offering the only answer to the growing threat to world wide 'food security', it appears that we are in danger of taking what, in some respects, might seem like a sensible route to follow, but without exploring other options along the way. A shift toward reliance upon GM as an answer to future food shortage concerns, carries with it an inherent danger. Regardless of any potential harm to the human body emanating from untested genetic modification, the more immediate harm can be seen in a revision of enclosure. Just as landowners carved up the commons for their own benefit and excluded those who formerly worked that land, the large seed producing companies are able to exclude farmers and growers through rigorous intellectual property rights legislation. Farmers and growers are forced to buy new seed each year as traditional methods and practises such as mutual seed exchange are outlawed.

Following the end of the Second World War, the food system in this country underwent massive change as new technologies, both mechanical and chemical, became available and were put to use on the land. It developed as part of a complex and convoluted global food system born out of what was to become known as the Green Revolution. At the time, the notion of a 'silent spring' was barely considered, but lessons learned through state control of the food system under rationing, together with the total embrace of the latest technologies, arguably led to the country being better-fed than it ever had been before. The perils of that new technology however, the pesticides and chemical fertilizers, were not explored at the time, and came at great cost to the environment. In order to avoid similar pitfalls, we clearly need a deeper understanding of how food systems work. That understanding needs to be entrenched, not just at a governmental level, but, more importantly, at an individual level too. That way, citizens will be better informed, and can make informed choices and decisions when deciding which way to vote each time the opportunity to change government comes around. There is a need, championed by the food heroes of today, for us all to better develop our insight into where food comes from, how it is produced, together with the environmental and social impact of that production.

We need to rethink our food systems. In the same way that fossil fuel companies wield control over the climate change agenda, and arms manufacturers clearly benefit from a deficit of world peace, the multinational food companies and the giant supermarket chains appear to have a firm grip on the global food system of today. In particular, the latter group are able to strengthen that hold by feeding directly into the food poverty agenda. Their apparently 'benevolent' redistribution of the mountains of food waste generated by the current food system amounts to little more than the corporatization of food poverty. It's not a solution. The creation of a secondary food market used to feed those who do not enjoy the economic access to food laid down in the declaration of the right to food, must surely be seen as a symptom of a failing food system. It's difficult to say whether this broken food system will lead directly to the re-occurrence of all-out food riots in this country once more, but I for one believe it is a distinct possibility. The valiant efforts of those involved in providing food charity in its various forms up and down the country, provide a relief which makes it somewhat unlikely, but it is a balance which may be easily upset in an age when more and more families appear to be falling below the poverty line. The hungry may once again be called to action at the sign of a loaf raised on a stick.

END NOTES

1. Jones, O. *Chavs, The Demonisation of the Working Class*, Verso London 2011, p 249.

BIBLIOGRAPHY

Archer, J.E. *Social Unrest and Popular Protest in England 1780-1840* (Cambridge: Cambridge University Press, 2000).

Beveridge, W.H. *British Food Control* (London, 1928).

Bjerga, A. *Endless Appetites: how the commodities casino creates hunger and unrest* (New Jersey: Bloomberg Press, 2011).

Bohstedt, J. *The Politics of Provisions: food riots, moral economy and market transition in England* (Farnham, Ashgate, 2010).

Bohstedt, J. *Riots and Community politics in England & Wales 1790-1810* (Harvard: Harvard University Press, 1983).

Bookchin, M. & Forman, D. *Defending the Earth - a dialogue*, (Boston: South End Press, 1991).

Briggs, A. *The Age of Improvement* (Harlow: Longman, 2000).

Burnett, J. *Plenty & Want: a social history of diet in England from 1815 to the present day* (London: Scolar Press, 1979).

Burchardt, J. *The Allotment Movement in England 1793-1873* (Woodbridge, 2002).

Cannon, G. *The Politics of Food* (London: Century Hutchinson Ltd, 1987).

Chambers, J. *Wiltshire Machine Breakers: the story of the 1830 riots Volume 1: The Riots & Trials* (Stamford, 2009).

Charlesworth, A. *An Atlas of Rural Protest in Britain 1548-1900* (London: Croon Helm, 1983). Cobbett, W (1830), *Rural Rides* (London: Penguin, 2001).

Collingham, L. *The Taste of War: World War Two and the battle for food* (London: Allen Lane, 2011).

Colquhoun, K. *Taste: the story of Britain through its cooking* (London: Bloomsbury, 2007).

Darke, N. *The Riot (a play)* (London, 1999).

Drummond, J.C. & Wilbraham, A. *The Englishman's Food: five centuries of English diet* (London: Jonathan Cape Ltd, 1939).

Dyck, I. *William Cobbett and rural popular culture* (Cambridge: Cambridge University Press, 1992).

Englander, D. *Poverty and Poor Law Reform in Nineteenth Century Britain 1834-1914* (London: Longman, 1998).

Fergusson, J. *The Vitamin Murders: who killed healthy eating in Britain?* (London: Portobello Books, 2007).

Griffin, C.J. *The Rural War, Captain Swing and the Politics of Protest* (Manchester: Manchester University Press, 2012).

Hamilton Jenkin, A. K. *Cornwall and its People* (London: JM Dent & Sons, 1946).

Hammond, J.L. & Hammond, B. *The Village Labourer 1760-1832* (London: Longman, 1911).

Hill, C. P. *British Economic and Social History, 1700 – 1939* (London: Edward Arnols, 1957).

Hobsbawm, E.J. *Industry and Empire* (Harmondsworth: Penguin, 1969).

Hobsbawm, E.J. & Rude, G. *Captain Swing* (London: Penguin, 1969).

Horspool, D. *The English Rebel: one thousand years of troublemaking from the Normans to the Nineties* (London: Viking, 2009).

Ingrams, R. *The Life and Adventures of William Cobbett* (London: Harper Collins, 2005).

Johnson, C. *An account of the Ely & Littleport Riots in 1816*, Harris & Sons, Littleport (volume reproduced by the Littleport Society www.littleportsociety.org.uk).

Jones, O. *Chavs - the demonization of the working class* (London: Verso, 2011).

Kingsford, P.W. *The Hunger Marches in Britain 1920-1939* (London: Lawrence & Wishart, 1982).

May, T. *The Economy 1815-1914*, (London: Collins, 1972).

Monbiot, G. *Captive State: the corporate takeover of Britain* (London: Macmillan, 2000).

Muskett, P. *Riotous Assemblies: popular disturbances in East Anglia* (Ely, 1984).

Palmer, R. (ed). *A Touch on the Times: songs of social change 1770 to 1914* (London: Penguin, 1974).

Palmer, R. *The Sound of History: songs & social comment* (London: Penguin, 1988).

Peacock, A.J. *Bread or Blood: a study of the agrarian riots in East Anglia in 1816* (London: Victor Gollancz, 1965).

Phillip, A.J. *Rations, Rationing and Food Control* (London, 1918).

Plumb, J.H. *England in the Eighteenth Century (1714-1815)* (Harmondsworth: Penguin, 1950).

Randall, A. *Riotous Assemblies; popular protest in Hanovarian England* (Oxford: Oxford University Press, 2006).

Randall, A. & Charlesworth, A. (eds). *Markets, Market Culture and Popular Protest in Eighteenth Century Britain* (Liverpool: Liverpool University Press, 1996).

Riches, G. & Silvasti, T. (eds). *First World Hunger Revisited* (London: Palgrave

Macmillan, 2014).

Rodway, A.E. & De Sola Pinto, V. (eds). *The Common Muse: popular British ballad poetry from the 15ᵗʰ to the 20ᵗʰ century* (London: Penguin, 1965).

Rose, M.E. *The Relief of Poverty, 1834-1914*, (London: Macmillan, 1972).

Shelton, W. J. *English Hunger and Industrial Disorders* (London: Macmillan, 1973).

Storey, N. *What Price Cod - a tugmaster's view of the Cod Wars* (Beverley: Hutton Press, 1992).

Tansey, G, & Rajotte, T. (eds). *The Future Control of Food* (London: Earthscan, 2008).

Tate, W.E. *The English Village Community and the Enclosure Movements*, (London: Victor Gollancz, 1967).

Thane, P. *Foundations of the Welfare State* (London: Longman 1982).

Thompson, D. *England in the Nineteenth Century* (Harmondsworth: Penguin, 1950).

Thompson, E.P. *The Making of the English Working Class* (Harmondsworth: Penguin, 1968).

PERIODICALS

De Chatel, F. 'The Role of Drought and Climate Change in the Syrian Uprising: Untangling the Triggers of the Revolution', *Middle Eastern Studies, L/4 (2014)*.

Fairlie, S. 'A Short History of Enclosure in Britain', *The Land Magazine*, Summer (2009).

Hussey, S. 'The Changing Face of Essex Gleaning', *The Agricultural History Review*. xxxiv/1. (1997).

King, P. 'Legal change, customary right and social conflict in the late 18th century', *Law and History*, x/1 (1992).

Osborne, S. & Winstanley, M. 'Rural and Urban Poaching in Victorian England', *Rural History*, xvii/2 (2006).

Randall, A. 'The Gloucestershire Food Riots of 1766', *Midlands History*, x/1 (1985).

Thompson, E.P. 'Rough Music Reconsidered', *Folklore*, Vol. Ciii/1 (1992).

Thompson, E.P. 'The Moral Economy of the English Crowd in the Eighteenth Century', *Past and Present*, 50 (1971), pp. 76-136.

Wells, R, 'William Cobbett and rural popular culture', *Agricultural History Review*, xxxv/1 (1997).

REPORTS AND PAPERS

DERFA, *Family Food Report*, ONS, (2012).

Eco Nexus Report 2013 - Agropoly; a handful of corporations control world food.

House of Commons, Environment, Food and Rural Affairs Committee, 'Food Security Second Report of Session 2014–15'. July 2014.

House of Commons, Environment, Food and Rural Affairs Committee, Securing Food Supplies up to 2050: fourth report of session, July,2009

Hossain, N., Brito, L., Jahan, F., Joshi, A., Nyamu-Musembi, C., Patnaik, B., Sambo, M., Shankland, A., Scott-Villiers, P., Sinha, D., Kalita, D. and Benequista, N. (2014) '"Them Belly Full (But We Hungry)": Food rights struggles in Bangladesh, India, Kenya and Mozambique.'

Synthesis report from DFID-ESRC research project 'Food Riots and Food Rights.' Brighton: Institute of Development Studies.

Schoen, V. & Lang,T. UK Food Prices: cooling or bubbling?, Food Research Collaboration (2014)

Fabian Society, A Recipe for Inequality - why our food system is leaving low income *households behind*, (2015)

Fabian Society, *Hungry for Change*, (2015)

ONLINE REFERENCES

www.newlynarchive.org.uk

www.west-penwith.org.uk

www.britishnewspaperarchive.co.uk

http://www.efdss.org/library-and-archive

http://freepages.family.rootsweb.ancestry.com/~treevecwll/riots.htm (The Acorn Archive)

Carew, R. Survey of Cornwall (1602) read online: http://www.gutenberg.org/

http://www.nationalarchives.gov.uk/records/research-guides/farm-survey.htm

http://www.workhouses.org.uk

http://web.utk.edu/~bohstedt/files/RCV_1766-1767.pdf

http://www.burbage-wiltshire.co.uk/historic/swing.html

http://www.swingriotsriotersblacksheepsearch.com

http://seedmagazine.com/content/article/food_fight_round_1/

http://seedmagazine.com/content/article/food_fight_round_2/

http://www.twnside.org.sg/title/twr118c.htm

http://www.worldhunger.org/articles/09/editorials/holt-gimenez.htm

http://theguardian.com/environment/damian-carrington-blog/2011/aug/25/
food-price-arab-middle-east-protests?

http://necsi.edu/research/social/food_crises.pdf

http://henryjacksonsociety.org/wp-content/uploads/2012/04/
Shocks-and-Disruptions-The-Relationship-Between-Food-Security-and-
National-Security.pdf

http://foodpovertyinquiry.org

http://church-poverty.org.uk/foodfuelfinance

http:/oxfam.org.uk/policyandpractice

http://www.historyextra.com/feature/1848-year-revolutions

http://www.thelandmagazine.org.uk/articles/short-history-enclosure-britain

http://foodwastecollective.blogspot.co.uk

http://www.carrotmuseum.co.uk/history4.html#disney

http://peopleshistreh.files.wordpress.com/2011/04/cheese_riots_complete_
displayversion.pdf

http://www.adamsmith.org

INDEX

NORTHERN COLLEGE LIBRARY
BARNSLEY S75 3ET
NC18961